Places to Go with Children

IN

NORTHERN CALIFORNIA

Elizabeth Pomada

Chronicle Books • San Francisco

Printed in the United States of America.

Library of Congress Cataloging in Publication Data
Pomada, Elizabeth.
   Places to go with children in northern California / Elizabeth Pomada.
   p. cm.
   ISBN 0-87701-544-9
   1. California, Northern—Description and travel—Guide-books. 2. Family recreation—California, Northern—Guide-books. I. Title.
F867.5.P66 1989
917.94'0453—dc19   88-39690
                                                                CIP

Editing: Carolyn Miller
Book and cover design: Seventeenth Street Studios
Composition: Another Point, Inc.

10 9 8 7 6 5 4 3 2

Chronicle Books
275 Fifth Street
San Francisco, California
94103

Needless to say, this book was not created by just one person. I must say "thank you" to Lauren and Jennifer, Elizabeth and Deborah, Diana and Marc, Eric and Chris, Cindy and Christopher and Alan, our "test" children. But most of all, thank you to my pal, editor, chauffeur, idea man, hero, and the biggest child of them all—MFL.

Contents

A Word Before You Go

Here, bigger and we hope better than ever, is the sixth edition of *Places to Go with Children in Northern California*. The countryside is as gorgeous and varied as ever, and it was a pleasure exploring it again, both to check on places already in the book and to find new discoveries to share with you.

Maybe it's just provincial pride, but we think that the ocean, rivers, trees, sunshine, mountains, and all of the breathtaking beauty and richness that Northern California has been blessed with make it one of the most beautiful areas on earth. More remarkable still is that so much of it has been protected or left in its natural state for us to marvel at.

We were pleased to find that the interest in preserving the state's colorful historical heritage continues to gain momentum. More museums and historic houses dot the landscape than ever. We believe that if you and your children can learn something and have fun at the same time, then the good time is worth twice as much. Most of the places listed here are enjoyable no matter how old you are.

Practically all of the places in *Places* have wheelchair access—indicated with a "W" at the end of the entries—and almost all of the attractions with educational value present special tours for school and other groups.

Most of the nonprofit institutions have gift shops, the sales from which help to sustain museums and nature centers. If you are pleased with what you see, these shops are one way of showing your support.

Most of the nonprofit attractions are staffed largely by volunteers. If you live in the area, another way of showing your support and making new friends is by helping out. Some places even have volunteer programs for children, which will be learning experiences for the kids and might even lead to a career.

The goal of *Places* is to include every attraction and special event in Northern California that children will enjoy. Since we concentrate on places to see rather than things to do, we've haven't included activities such as bowling, skateboarding, skiing, pool, skating, miniature golf, ballooning, etc. If we mention a water slide or airport in one area, for example, and that sounds like a good idea to you, check your local Yellow Pages to see if there's one nearby. One adventure may lead to another.

We hope that you will help make the next edition even better. Please write to me at 1029 Jones Street, San Francisco, 94109, or call me at (415) 673-0939 if you find an attraction that should be in the next edition, or if you think of a way to make *Places* more meaningful to parents and teachers. We will be happy to acknowledge your suggestion in the book and send an autographed copy of the new edition to the first person to suggest a new place to visit or one we have overlooked.

If you have any unusual experience, good or bad, at the places in the book, we would like to know about them. Also, if your children or students write anything memorable about the places they visit, we'd like to see it—and perhaps quote them in the next edition. We would like to make *Places* a dialogue so that it will continue to improve.

Schedules and prices do change, especially in winter and holidays, so, if you're going far, call for up-to-the-minute information and driving and lodging tips. Local Chambers of Commerce, tourist offices, and the American Automobile Association will also help you plan your trip. And don't forget to stock the car with travel snacks and games, books and books on tape, tissues, disposable towels, and a lot of good humor.

We hope that you will enjoy *Places* and the places it inspires you to visit. *Bon Voyage!*

Northern California's Top 11 Places

1. Monterey Aquarium
2. San Francisco Exploratorium
3. Yosemite National Park
4. Oakland Museum
5. Marine World Africa USA, Vallejo
6. Santa Cruz Boardwalk
7. Lawrence Hall of Science, Berkeley
8. San Francisco Zoo
9. California State Railroad Museum, Old Sacramento
10. Point Reyes National Seashore
11. Great America, Santa Clara

To which I add my personal favorites:
1. John Muir House, Martinez
2. Columbia State Historic Park
3. San Juan Bautista State Historic Park
4. Winchester Mystery House, San Jose
5. Rosicrucian Museum, San Jose
6. Zalud House, Porterville
7. House of Happy Walls, Jack London State Historic Park, Glen Ellen
8. Lachyrma Montis, General Vallejo's Home, Sonoma State Historic Park
9. San Francisco Historic Ships at Hyde Street Pier.

San Francisco and the Bay Area

San Francisco

San Francisco has been called a peninsula bounded on three sides by water and one side by reality. What makes the City special? It's both large and small. At about 750,000 people, it's small for a major city. Yet it has the amenities of any great city: opera, ballet, theater, a symphony, shopping galore, and restaurants that will please any palate.

San Francisco is a unique blend of qualities:
☐ a beautiful natural setting
☐ cool but fair weather
☐ a history that makes up in color for what it lacks in length
☐ a rich multicultural heritage that makes the city hospitable to new people, ideas, and lifestyles
☐ old and new architecture, including the greatest and most beautiful collection of redwood Victorians in the world
☐ distinct neighborhoods worth wandering in
☐ a world-class mixture of education, business, culture, and religion that attracts visitors and immigrants from all over the world
☐ a size small enough to walk around in yet large enough to provide kids of all ages with plenty of things to see and do.

Consider transportation. You can see San Francisco by foot, bicycle, moped, car, taxi, bus (single or double decker), cable car (regular or motorized), trolley car, subway, helicopter, ferry, sailboat, and even blimp!

The Golden Gate Bridge provides a dramatic backdrop for walkers, joggers, and dreamers.

Hungry? San Francisco provides an excellent opportunity to expand your children's enjoyment of the world's cuisine. The first ten blocks of Clement Street in the Richmond District offer the most cosmopolitan concentration of delectable food we know of anywhere. Here, you can feast on Chinese food (including *dim sum* and Cantonese, Mandarin, and Hunan-style cooking), and Japanese, Italian, Indonesian, French, Russian, Persian, Vietnamese, Irish, Thai, barbecue, natural foods, and even American food!

San Francisco suffers from the same problems as any metropolis, but the City's size, human-scale architecture (outside of our mini-Manhattan downtown), and sunny weather give urban blight a more benign quality.

The City has a remarkable capacity for self-renewal. Although still largely populated by the poor and the nefarious, the Tenderloin is being revitalized by Vietnamese refugees. Kids are playing in the streets, stores and restaurants have sprouted up, and the area is adding another neighborhood to the City's rich ethnic mix.

Much of the best of what the City has to offer is free. More than one-third of the attractions in this chapter are free. San Francisco is a walker's paradise. Just strolling around Golden Gate Park or the City's neighborhoods—Chinatown, Japantown, the Mission, Noe Valley, Clement Street, Union Street, or anywhere on the waterfront from Land's End to the Embarcadero—on a sunny, breezy day is delightful. For views, try the free ride on the outside elevator to the Crown Room at the top of the Fairmont Hotel, one of the best free rides in the world. Or stop by Coit Tower on the top of Telegraph Hill. The observation platform at the top is 210 feet high (open daily, 9–4:30).

Unless you hit one of the City's few hot days, the temperature is usually in the low sixties. So the layered look, which enables you to peel off a jacket or sweater if it gets toasty, is always appropriate.

The "Pinkie," the pink section in the Sunday *Chronicle,* will fill you in on special events that are taking place while you are in town.

Whether you live in the City or are just visiting, whether you are young or just young at heart, whether you want cultural enrichment or just plain fun, San Francisco is one of the best places in the world to spend a week or a lifetime. So as they say these days: "Go for it!"

Golden Gate Ferry to Larkspur or Sausalito

Next to the Ferry Building at the foot of Market Street. (415) 332-6600. Ferries leave the City daily. Call for schedule. Sausalito: Adults, $3.70; children, $2.80. Larkspur: Adults $4.40; children $3.30.

The Golden Gate Ferry leaves its slip at the foot of Market Street, passes Alcatraz Island, and docks across the bay. The shop on board serves good coffee and snacks, and whether it's sunny or foggy the views are wonderful! Bring a camera.

The Sailing Ship Restaurant
Pier 42–44, Berry Street at the Embarcadero. (415) 777-5771.

The *Dolphin P. Rempp,* one of the last of the three-masted topsail schooners to ply the Pacific trade, is now open for dinner and Sunday brunch. While dining on fine Continental cuisine you can "pretend sail" on a ship you saw in *Hawaii* or *Mutiny on the Bounty* and see super views of the bay.

World of Oil
555 Market Street. (415) 894-4895. Monday–Friday, 9:30–4. Films weekdays at noon. Group tours by appointment. W. Free.

If you've ever wondered how oil is found, produced, transformed into thousands of products, and used for energy, heat, and lubrication, this is the place to come. Tapes, films, an energy quiz, and interactive displays show junior scientists how oil was obtained and used in the past. Photos, drilling and rigging tools, and models of offshore wells are eye-openers. Three life-sized dioramas show the role oil has played in American life. The first service station and the 1910 kitchen have a nostalgic appeal.

The Old U.S. Mint
Fifth and Mission streets. (415) 974-0788. Tuesday–Saturday 10–4. Closed on holidays. Tours by appointment. Free.

The Granite Lady, a half-hour film, shows the history of California and the part the Old Mint has played in it, from the crackling excitement of the Gold Rush to the terror of the 1906 earthquake and fire. Visitors can see tokens, bank notes, walrus and sealskins, and other forms of money, as well as a stack of 128 gold bars and gold nuggets. In the superintendent's office, the clock reads "Time Is Money." Visitors can strike their own souvenir medal on an 1869 coil press during their 90-minute tour.

San Francisco has several fountains that invite the viewer to be a participant. The Vaillancourt Fountain, at the foot of Market Street, is a favorite. Here youngsters enjoy jumping over the rocks of the mountain-streamlike Monumental Fountain, designed by Lawrence Halprin for Levi Plaza on San Francisco's Embarcadero.

The Asawa Fountain

Hyatt Hotel on Union Square. Stockton Street between Sutter and Post. Free.

Ruth Asawa, artist and creator of the Mermaid Fountain in Ghirardelli Square, has given the people of San Francisco a one-stop tour of the City. This fountain, 14 feet in diameter, on the steps of the plaza of the Hyatt Hotel on Union Square, was molded in bread dough—the same dough children use for sculpting—and cast in bronze. And the little people, trees, Chinese dragon, Painted Ladies, and school buses demand to be touched. At the bottom of the fountain is the Ferry Building; as you go around it, you'll see Coit Tower, Broadway, Aquatic Park, the Cannery, the zoo, the Mission district—everything laid out in the same general direction as it is in real life. A group of Noe Valley schoolchildren created one of the fountain's 41 plaques, which depicts the children of San Francisco. Your kids will enjoy figuring out which one it is.

Museum of Money of the American West
Bank of California, 400 California Street, downstairs. (415) 765-0400. Monday–Thursday 10–3, Friday until 5. Free.

This small but nicely mounted collection of money and gold provides a glimpse of banking and mining in the Old West. Each coin is a piece of history. Privately minted coins from Utah, Colorado, and California show the kind of money used before the U.S. Mint was set up in San Francisco. Ingots, gold bullion, currency, and early bank drafts are here, along with counterfeit coins and counterfeit detectors. One method of counterfeiting, "the platinum menace," hollowed out coins and filled them with platinum, then worth much less than gold. Is that why an Oregon two-ounce copper alloy coin reads "In Gold We Trust?"

Wells Fargo History Room
420 Montgomery Street. (415) 396-2619. Banking days 9–5. Guided tours by appointment. Free. W.

Ever wanted to bounce along in a stagecoach? Or send a telegraph message? Or rock a gold-panning cradle? The youngsters can relive the romance of the west in this beautifully designed bi-level museum. Here you'll find gold, money, treasure boxes, art, tools, photos, a map of Black Bart's 28 stagecoach robberies, iron doors from a Wells Fargo office in Gold Country, Pony Express memorabilia, and a rocking Concord Stage Coach with an audiotape of one young man's trip from St. Louis to San Francisco. A videotape shows how Wells Fargo commercials, starring the bank's symbol, a stagecoach, are made and how today's stagecoaches are made with century-old tools.

Museum of Modern Mythology
693 Mission Street. (415) 546-0202. Thursday–Saturday 12–5. Donation.

This showplace for 20th-century artifacts of pop and schlock culture, featuring advertising memorabilia, is very amusing. There's Elsie the Borden

The Cable Car is the favorite mode of transportation in San Francisco for children of all ages. This one is stopped at Old St. Mary's Church at California Street and Grant Avenue.

Cow, Disneyana, the Pillsbury Dough Boy, the head of Doggie Diner, and two polyester shirts, all advertising something.

Chinatown

A visit to San Francisco would not be complete without a visit to Chinatown, along Grant Avenue from Bush to Broadway or along Stockton from Sacramento to Vallejo. For the curious, there are fortune cookie factories, fish stores, and temples, as well as shops and restaurants.

The **Golden Gate Fortune Cookie Factory** on Ross Alley, between Washington and Jackson, above Grant, sometimes leaves its doors open so you can see the row of tiny griddles revolving under a hose that squirts dough onto each pan. The pans cook the dough on their way to the cookie-maker, who picks up each browned wafer, pushes it into a spur for the first fold, inserts the paper fortune, presses the final fold, and puts the cookie in a muffin tin to harden. For more than a peek, make an appointment at 731-3956.

T'ien Hou Miao Temple (125 Waverly, Fourth Floor; 10–5 and 7–9 p.m. daily) is dedicated to the Queen of Heaven and boasts a ceiling filled with carved wood mythological figures. Just follow the scent of incense up the stairs.

One of our favorite lunchtime meals is *dim sum*. *Dim sum*, also called Chinese tea or tea lunch, means "heart's delights," and there's always something to entice every taste. *Dim sum* is simply little bites of good things. A waitress comes around with a cart from which you choose small plates of such delicacies as shrimp rolls, curry cakes, beef dumplings, spareribs, mushroom turnovers, or steamed barbecued pork buns, *bao*. If your choice is on two plates, and there are only two of you, ask for a half order. You pay for the number of dishes chosen. In Chinatown, we recommend the **Hong Kong Tea Garden** on Pacific and the **Golden Dragon** on Washington, both between Stockton and Grant, and the **Grand Palace** on Grant.

Cultural, historical, and artistic exhibitions are presented in **The Chinese Cultural Center**, the forum for the Chinese community (750 Kearny, in the Holiday Inn, third floor; 415-986-1822; daily 10–4; free).

*The colorful buildings of San Francisco's
Chinatown enhance the area's exotic
appeal.*

Chinese Historical Society of America

*7 Alder Place (between Grant and Columbus, just south of Broadway,
around the corner from City Lights Bookstore). (415) 391-1188. Tuesday–
Saturday 1–5. Donation.*

Chinese societies throughout California have contributed to this small, hidden museum to show the role played by the Chinese in California's development. Ceremonial swords, printing blocks, an altar, porcelain pillows, clothes worn by 19th-century laborers and the high-born, opium pipes, photographs, and documents crowd the display space. A shrimp cleaner leads the way downstairs to changing exhibits such as one on the first women to vote in America or another on the first telephone system in San Francisco.

North Beach Museum

1435 Stockton Street, upstairs in Eureka Federal Savings Bank. (415) 334-4600. Monday–Friday 9–4:30. Tours by appointment. Free.

Photographs and artifacts in changing thematic exhibits celebrate the City's, and especially North Beach's, colorful past, from the Gold Rush to the Earthquake, to the growth of the neighborhood as the center of the City's Italian community, to the Beat Generation.

Cable Car Barn Museum

1201 Mason Street at Washington. (415) 474-1887. Daily 10–5:45. Closed holidays. Donation.

All three cable car lines in San Francisco are run by the huge revolving red and yellow wheels in the brick cable car barn, built in 1887. Visitors can watch the wheels from a gallery, where there are samples of the cable itself and charts explaining how the cable cars work. You can see scale models, Earthquake mementos, old cable car seats, and photographs and cable cars on display, including the first one to operate in San Francisco, in 1873. An exciting underground viewing room lets you see the cables running under the city streets from the car barn at 9½ miles an hour. A 16-minute video offers more information.

Society of California Pioneers

456 McAllister Street. (415) 861-5278. Monday–Friday, 10–4. Free.

A Gold Rush California exhibit, including early San Francisco silver coins, 19th-century paintings, and a Wells Fargo stagecoach, brings eager visitors. We're fond of the Earthquake slide show with special effects.

San Francisco Museum of Modern Art

War Memorial Veterans Building, Van Ness at McAllister. (415) 863-8800. Tuesday–Friday 10–5, Thursday until 9, weekends 11–5. Adults $3.50; children under 16, $1.50; free Tuesday 10–5; reduced rates Thursday night and for groups.

The Museum of Modern Art offers constantly changing exhibits of paintings, sculpture, works of art on paper, and photography. Ceramics and graphics are part of the permanent art collection, which emphasizes modern masters such as San Franciscans Wayne Thiebaud and Clyfford Still. There are many who feel that children are best able to view modern art because they're open to everything, with no preconceived ideas about what art should be. While looking at a room full of Jonathan Borofsky's *Chattering Men*, we were inclined to agree.

The Hard Rock Cafe

1699 Van Ness, at Sacramento, (415) 885-1699. 11:30–11:30 daily, until 12:30 Fri. & Sat. Reservations for lunch only. Valet parking on Sacramento. W.

Don't ask your kids where they'd like to eat unless you're prepared to come here. The Hard Rock Cafe is just as much a rock and roll shrine as it is a restaurant. It's a mecca for rock fans of all ages. Sounds of the great rockers greet you as you walk into a large, two-level room, the walls of which are covered with posters, gold and platinum records, and the guitars of rock greats. The room has a California openness punctuated by a dodge 'em car, a motorcycle, and a standard Hard-Rock fixture: half of a Cadillac over the entranceway. The menu's California touches lighten the load of affordable golden oldies like ribs, fries, hamburgers, shakes and banana splits. On the way out, your kids may insist on stopping at the boutique to buy the most visible form of institutional advertising in the world: a souvenir T-Shirt. Expect a wait at busy times, which are most times.

Haas-Lilienthal House

2007 Franklin Street between Washington and Jackson. (415) 441-3004. Guided tours Wednesday at 3:15, Sunday 11–4. Adults $3, students and seniors $1. Groups by appointment.

This glorious Queen Anne Victorian, built in 1886, is a completely furnished memory of yesterday, right down to the cat on the sofa. Children of all ages will especially enjoy the train room.

Ghirardelli Chocolate Manufactory

Ghirardelli Square, 900 North Point, between Polk and Larkin. (415) 771-4903. 11:30–10 daily, later in summer.

Since the beginning of the century, Ghirardelli Stoneground Chocolate has been a popular trade name throughout the west. This red-brick, aromatic ice cream and candy shop invokes that name in a nostalgic corner of the old Ghirardelli factory. After filling out an order form and paying the cashier, you locate a marble-topped table, then take turns watching the chocolate-making machine in the back of the room until your order number is called. We always imagine what it would be like diving into the big vats where the chocolate is conched after the beans are roasted, cracked, husked, ground, and mixed with other ingredients. Instead, we dive into a hot fudge sundae, or a delicious extravaganza like the Emperor Norton, with bananas, or the Chocolate Decadence. Or we opt for a soda or cone.

The square itself is three stories full of stores and restaurants, many with great views of the bay. Here you can find shoes, popcorn, cookies, crafts, books, perfume, clothes, and gifts galore. Jugglers and street entertainers perform on weekends and in summer.

The American Carousel Museum

633 Beach Street, across from the Cannery. (415) 928-0550. Daily 10–5, until 6 in summer. Adults $2, seniors $1, under 12 free. Tours by appointment. W.

A Wurlitzer Band organ plays lively carousel music as you walk through this well-designed display of beautiful carousel animals. The restoration room shows horses in varying stages of carving, restoring, and painting, and visitors can watch, or help with, the work in progress. Here you can see the difference between an English carousel horse, which moves clockwise, and an American one, which moves counter-clockwise: the elaborate jewelry, "the Romance side," is always on the side facing out. We fell in love with the pink and green dragon sea horse.

*Girls love building trucks with the Brio
set at the San Francisco International Toy
Museum.*

San Francisco International Toy Museum
*2801 Leavenworth Street in the Cannery. (415) 441-TOYS. Daily, 10–6,
Adults $3; children over 5 $2; students and seniors $1.*

Kids of all ages are encouraged to relax and unwind as they play together
on games, building toys, ride-in trucks and fire engines, 100,000 Leggos,
stuffed animals, dolls, trains, and more in the Playspace of this dream-
come-true museum. A museum, The Celebration of Toys, is across the hallway, showing unique toys from all over the world, and over the ages. There
are antique tin toys that survived the Earthquake, puppets, toy motorcy-
cles, and rotating collections. Most of the toys have been donated by toy
stores, toy companies, and people who want to share the joy of childhood

Dollhouses and foam bats and balls are some of the many attractions at the San Francisco International Toy Museum.

with others. This museum is the only one of its kind in the world, the successful vision of its passionate founder, Dr. Stevanne Auerbach.

Naturally, since the Cannery is a shopping complex, there are many gift and crafts stores and restaurants to browse through. Our favorite is *3 Cheers Cafe,* open from breakfast through dinner for snacks, coffee, fresh carrot or orange juice, or full California-fresh meals. The spectacular view out the window-wall ranges from the Golden Gate Bridge to the Berkeley hills.

National Maritime Museum at San Francisco (GGNRA)
Foot of Polk Street on Beach. (415) 556-8177. Daily 10–5, until 6 in summer. Call for calendar of events. W. Free.

The Maritime Museum is a mecca for ship lovers of all ages. The maritime history of San Francisco lives on here in models of clippers, British iron ships, schooners, barkentines, cutters, and cod fishers; and in photos, figureheads, tools, scrimshaw, guns and harpoons, diaries, and ships' logs. The 19-foot sloop *Mermaid,* which one man sailed from Osaka to San Francisco, is on the veranda. Billy Bones and Anne Bonny are two of the pirates standing at the entrance to the Steamship Room. Inside, you'll see models of the *Queen Mary,* along with cargo and warships from World War I to the present.

San Francisco Historic Ships at Hyde Street Pier (GGNRA)
Hyde Street Pier at Aquatic Park. (415) 556-6435. Daily 10–5, later in summer. Tours and Environmental Living Programs by appointment. Limited wheelchair access.

The Balclutha, one of the last surviving square-rigged Cape Horners, is berthed at the Hyde Street Pier. You can spin the wheel, visit the "slop chest" and galley, check out the captain's quarters with its swinging bed, ring bells, and read sea chanties and rousing tales of the Barbary Coast below decks, while the movement of the boat on the water heightens the imagination.

You can also go below decks on the *C. A. Thayer,* a salmon packet, to see the captain's family cabin. There are antique cars waiting for the next docking on the ferryboat *Eureka.* And you can check out the *Alma,* the last remaining San Francisco bay scow schooner, or the six-room *Lewis Ark* houseboat. Other boats are docked on occasion, such as the paddle tug *Eppleton Hall* or the steam schooner *Wapama,* and some will be boardable. On land, there are engine room showings, boat-building classes, movies and videos, and changing exhibits.

Guinness Museum of World Records
235 Jefferson Street at Fisherman's Wharf. (415) 771-9890. Sunday–Thursday 10–10, Friday and Saturday until midnight. Adults $5.95; children under 12, $2.75.

World records from the Guinness Book of World Records come to life in this curious museum. You'll be overwhelmed with record-setting objects, audience-participation displays, dramatizations, and multimedia videotapes and films of records being set. You can see the world's tallest man and the world's smallest book. A collection of the biggest, the smallest, and the mostest.

Ripley's Believe it or Not Museum
175 Jefferson Street, at Fisherman's Wharf. (415) 771-6188. Sunday–Thursday 10–10, Friday and Saturday until 12. Adults $5.95; children under 12 $2.75. School tours by appointment.

This three-story collection of over 2,500 oddities and puzzles is almost unbelievable. Did you know there was a real Mother Goose? Have you heard of the Lincoln log cabin made of 16,360 Lincoln pennies? When you walk down the Crooked Lane, you see strange things, from a man with two pupils in each eye to a display of "dressed" fleas.

Wax Museum at Fisherman's Wharf
145 Jefferson Street at Fisherman's Wharf. (415) 885-2023. Daily 10–10, Friday and Saturday 9:30 a.m.–11:30 p.m. Adults $6.95, seniors and military $4, children $2.95. Group rates.

Meet Prince Charles and Princess Diana, Abraham Lincoln, Mona Lisa, Michael Jackson, King Tut with his treasures, Elvis Presley, Peter Pan and Snow White, and more heroes and villians in four floors of scenes re-creating the past, present, and world of the future. The Chamber of Horrors on the lower level is "not recommended for cowards, sissys, and yellerbellies."

Lazermaze
107 Jefferson Street, across from Fisherman's Wharf. (415) 471-6349. Daily 10–10; later in summer and on weekends. $3. Group and party rates.

In the world's first walk-in video game, players may select from three skill levels in attempts to increase scores. In this fantasy world, you experience live laser combat against life-sized attack robots, and you have seconds to fire your laser blaster or else!

There's nothing like tackling a cracked crab on the spot at Fisherman's Wharf.

Commodore Helicopter Tours
Pier 43. (415) 981-4821. Daily 10—sunset, weather permitting. Adults $20; children under 10, $10 (for the 4-minute Bell Jet Ranger Ride). Charter rates available.

This exciting 125-mph ride swoops around Alcatraz, out onto the bay, and around the City for great views. Be sure to bring your camera. There are three tours to choose from.

U.S.S. Pampanito
Pier 45, near Fisherman's Wharf. (415) 929-0202. Daily 9—6, until 9 on weekends and in summer. Adults $3, juniors $2, children and seniors $1.

This World War II—vintage submarine is a floating museum and a memorial to the men who served in the "silent service." Self-guided tours through the cramped quarters are explained via audiotape.

Alcatraz Island (GGNRA)

Pier 41. (415) 392-7469. Frequent sailings on the Red and White fleet daily. Advance ticket purchase through Ticketron is strongly suggested. To cruise around the Rock on a Red and White Cruise tour narrated by Frank Heaney, a former prison guard, call (415) 546-2896. Boats leave Pier 41 regularly.

Wear walking shoes and bring a sweater on this educational, fascinating-yet-depressing self-guided walking tour of Alcatraz. One friend calls the two-hour trip a surefire way to stop juvenile delinquency.

Bay Cruises

*In California, call 1-800-445-8880 or (415) 546-2896. Boats leave from Pier 41 and 43½. The **Blue and Gold Fleet** out of Pier 39 has a 1¼ hour bay cruise. For schedules and prices, call (415) 781-7877. Group rates.*

On a sunny day in San Francisco, there's nothing nicer for the family than getting out on San Francisco Bay. You can take a ferry that goes to Sausalito, Angel Island, Tiburon, or Marine World, or simply take a guided-tour cruise of the bay, under the Golden Gate and Bay bridges. The **Red and White Fleet** offers a 45-minute cruise and six other choices.

The San Francisco Experience

Pier 39. (415) 982-7394. Daily, every half hour 10–10. Adults $4.50; ages 6–16 and military, $3. Group rates. School programs. W.

Seven screens, 32 speakers, three movie projectors, and 32 slide projectors bring you the spirit and history of San Francisco, from the gold mines to the building of the Golden Gate Bridge to the present. Experience the San Francisco Earthquake of 1906 and a Chinese New Year's parade. The San Francisco memorabilia, nickelodeons, and games make waiting in the lobby for the next show a pleasure.

Pier 39 is a shopping/restaurant complex set right on the water. There's a double-decker merry-go-round and a games arcade for the children. Sailing sessions and lessons and buggy and rickshaw rides are available. On weekends, street entertainers stroll the boards.

San Francisco Fire Department Museum

*655 Presidio, between Pine and Bush. (415) 861-8000, ext. 365. Thursday–
Sunday 1–4, and by appointment. W. Free.*

Awe-inspiring photos of today's firefighters mingle with uniforms, bells,
trophies and mementos of men and machines, a silver speaking trumpet,
leather buckets, a buffalo-leather firehose, and other relics of yesteryear.
Lillie Coit, the darling of the San Francisco Fire Department, has her own
case full of mementos. A 1912 fire chief's buggy, an 1890 American La-
France Steam Fire Engine, and other machinery fill the room.

The Whittier Mansion

*2090 Jackson Street. (415) 567-1848. Wednesday, Saturday, and Sunday,
tours at 1:30 and 3. Groups by appointment. Adults $3, students and seniors
$1. Free first Wednesday of the month.*

The 1896 Whittier Mansion, home of the California Historical Society, features revolving exhibits of California art. En route to the second-floor exhibit area, you pass through gracious drawing rooms with parquet floors,
handsome fireplaces, and carved wainscotting. The society offers changing
exhibits on the history, arts, and culture of California.

Japan Center

Post and Buchanan Streets. (415) 563-1030. W.

With stores and restaurants and the Japanese bowling alley across the
street, Japan Center, **Nihonmachi**, can really be another world. The Peace
Plaza with its reflecting pools and five-tiered Peace Pagoda is the center of
entertaining festivals and celebrations during the year. You can see music
and dance programs as well as judo, karate, and kendo matches. Inside the
center, you can fish for an oyster with a pearl in it, or have a Japanese fish-
shaped *tai yaki,* a warm, filled, wafflelike pastry. Kids like the Hello Kitty
store.

   Introduce the kids to sushi at **Isobune.** Here you sit in front of a circular
stream. Boats float by you carrying little plates of sushi. You take off what
looks good, and pay by the plate. Start with the *ebi,* cooked shrimp; the
tamago, or sweet omelet; or the California roll of crab and avocado. My
nephew was hooked on the *unagi,* broiled eel with a sweet sauce.

Fort Mason

Once a lonely barracks and deserted piers, Fort Mason, at the foot of Marina Boulevard and Laguna, is now a flourishing center for the arts. Nonprofit organizations from Greenpeace to Media Alliance are based here, and several performing arts groups give shows. **Greens**, an elegant vegetarian restaurant, has a phenomenal view of the docks, the bay, and the Golden Gate Bridge (771-6222 for lunch and dinner reservations). The San Francisco Museum of Modern Art's rental wing is in Building A, as is the Dorothy Weiss Gallery and Fort Mason Art Center. The following are of special interest to the young:

☐ **Museo Italo-Americano.** Building C; (415) 673-2200; Wednesday–Sunday 12–5 and by appointment W; free. Preserves and displays Italian and Italo-American art, history, and culture in changing exhibits. Classes, community activities, and films are presented.

☐ **San Francisco African-American Historical and Cultural Society.** Building C; (415) 441-0640. Tuesday–Saturday 12–5; school groups by appointment; W; free. African and Black American artists and inventors are honored in the exhibit hall of this group. Clothing, African artifacts, pottery, historical documents, and crafts are displayed. There are special rotating exhibits such as one on Black cowboys and another on Mammy Pleasant.

☐ **Mexican Museum.** Building D; (415) 441-0445; Wednesday–Sunday 12–5, Wednesday until 8; adults $4, students $2; free first Wednesday of the month. Pre-Hispanic, contemporary, and folk art by Mexicans and Chicanos make up the changing exhibits in this well-designed museum. Hands-on exhibits, student programs, and guided tours of the Mission district's murals are available.

☐ **Jeremiah O'Brien.** Pier 3 E; (415) 441-3101; weekends 11–4; adults $2, seniors and children $1; $5 per family; volunteers welcome; open Ship Celebration Weekends; group tours. The last of the Liberty Ships carried food and ammunition to England, ferried troops during the Normandy Invasion, and transported supplies to the South Pacific. Now it's back "home" where it was built, and has been restored to be shared with the public. On the third weekend of the month, the steam is up and the galley stove is working. Volunteers serve hot dogs, chocolate chip cookies, and lemonade, and kids can even blow the whistle.

Octagon House
2645 Gough Street at Union. (415) 885-9796. Second and fourth Thursday and second Sunday of each month, 12–3. Free.

Built in 1861, this unusual eight-sided home is the local headquarters of the National Society of the Colonial Dames of America as well as a gracious museum of Americana. A pack of Revolutionary War playing cards, a 13-star flag, dishes taken in battle by the U.S.S. *Constitution* and a 19th-century "mammy bench" make this a pleasantly educational stop.

Mission Dolores
Dolores at 16th Street. (415) 621-8203. Daily 10–4 in winter, 9–4:30 in summer. Adults and group tours, $1.

Built in 1776, the Mission San Francisco de Asis is the City's oldest structure. The Corinthian and Moorish architecture is not at all like that of the other California missions. The cemetery contains the remains of some of the City's first settlers.

Josephine D. Randall Junior Museum
199 Museum Way off Roosevelt, Upper Market Street area, at 15th Street, west of Castro. (415) 863-1399. Tuesday–Saturday 10–5. Free.

High on a sunny hill overlooking the city, this museum and zoo is especially designed for children. Here they can watch a seismograph, see dinosaur bones and eggs, learn about the California Indians, and pat a live chicken and goat. They can also talk to crows and magpies, handle various minerals and ores, and learn about electricity. During one Saturday visit, youngsters were helping to clean the cages while two plump raccoons played on the front lawn, and Puff the Iguana took an airing on the zoo keeper's arm. Members of the Golden Gate Model Railroad Club, located downstairs in the building, allow the public to watch them play with the model trains on the huge room-sized tract on occasional Friday nights.

Golden Gate Park
From Fulton and Stanyan Streets west to the ocean. The park office is in McLaren Lodge: 588-3706.

There are more than 1,000 acres of lakes and greenery in San Francisco's Golden Gate Park and at least 100 things to see and do. You can go boating or feed the ducks, cheer toy sailboat races, picnic, ride horses, play tennis, golf, or handball, go lawn bowling, watch the grazing buffalo, bicycle, skate, watch soccer and polo matches, pitch horseshoes, shoot arrows, play cards or chess, fly cast, or make water rings in the fountains. Stow Lake is the place to rent rowboats, motorboats, and pedal boats. Visit the magical, silvery Golden Gate pavilion from China, located on Stow Lake's island.

The Children's Playground, located on the Lincoln Avenue side of the park, features the slide with the fastest ride in the west, plus three other slides, geometrical shapes to climb, and swings.

The nearby **Herschel-Stillman 1912 Carousel** has been perfectly and wonderfully restored, with 62 menagerie animals, mostly in sets of two—cats, dogs, zebras, tigers, roosters, storks, giraffes, reindeer, frogs, pigs, goats, and beautiful horses—like Noah's Ark, plus a love-tub and a rocker. (Wednesday–Sunday 10–4:15; $1).

Older children might enjoy a walk through **Shakespeare's Garden** to identify the plants he wrote about. You can climb a moon bridge in the **Japanese Tea Garden** and then sit down to tea and cookies in the Tea House (Monday–Saturday 9–6:30; adults $1, children and seniors, 50¢; school tours: 558-4870).

Browse through the spun-sugar Victorian **Conservatory** on Kennedy Drive at any time of year to see displays of flowers in a tropical atmosphere (daily 9–4:30; 558–3983). Ring the Mexican Bell in the Strybing Arboretum's Garden of Fragrance, where you can test your sense of smell, touch, and taste (weekdays 8–4:30, weekends and holidays 10–5; tours at 1:30, theme walks on Saturdays at 1:30; 661-0668).

Gaze at the Portals of the Past, the marble columns that are all that was left of a Nob Hill mansion after the Earthquake and are now the guardians of a duck-filled lake. Don't forget to say thank you to John McLaren—his statue is tucked in a dell of rhododendrons across from the Conservatory although he hated statues in parks—for turning sand dunes into an oasis of greenery gracing the City.

M. H. de Young Memorial Museum
Golden Gate Park, north side of Music Concourse. (415) 221-4811. Wednesday–Sunday 10–5. Adults $4; over 65, $2; under 18, free. First Wednesday of the month free. One charge admits you to the de Young, Asian Art, and the Palace of Legion of Honor museums on the same day. Docent tours and school programs. W.

The de Young's romantic Pool of Enchantment, with water lilies and a sculpted boy playing his pipes to two mountains lions, beckons visitors to this land of enchantment. There are paintings, sculpture, tapestries, and graphics by American, Californian, and European artists. The Rembrandt is a favorite, and there is a lovely Mary Cassatt in the American section. The American Wing, donated by Mrs. John D. Rockefeller, houses the memorable *Rainy Season in the Tropics* by Frederick Church and several works by the Ash Can artists.

Children especially like the "real rooms": the muraled boudoir from Italy and the paneled Louis XV salon. Art from Africa, Oceania, and South America is not forgotten. A pleasant cafeteria and garden is open for lunch and afternoon tea.

Asian Art Museum, Avery Brundage Collection

Golden Gate Park, north side of Music Concourse. (415) 668-8921. Wednesday 10–8:45, Thursday–Sunday 10–5, Adults, $4; over 65, $2. Free 10–12 on Saturdays and the first Wednesday of each month. Tours by appointment. W.

Chinese galleries on the first floor display objects from prehistoric times to the 19th century, including a magnificent collection of jade in a jewel-box setting, the Magnin jade room. Second-floor galleries exhibit art from Japan, Korea, India, Southeast Asia, Tibet, Nepal, and Siam. Both floors overlook the Japanese Tea Garden at the west end.

California Academy of Sciences

Golden Gate Park, south side of Music Concourse. (415) 750-7145; taped information 750-7000. Daily 10–5 in winter, summer till 7. Adults $4;' ages 12–17, $2; ages 6–11, $1. Free the first Wednesday of the month. Rats for groups by appointment. W.

Wander through the innovative Wild California Hall, the Hall of Gems and Minerals, and the Hall of the North American Birds. Be sure to visit the Wattis Hall of Human Cultures, the African Safari Hall with sights and sounds of Africa, and the Earth and Space Hall with the Safe-Quake, a ride that simulates an earthquake. The Far Side of Science Gallery features the work of cartoonist Gary Larson.

Here you'll find **Morrison Planetarium**, a unique sky theater presenting a simulation of the heavens as seen from Earth at any time—past, present,

Friendly reptiles welcome visitors to the
California Academy of Science

or future—on the 65-foot hemispherical dome. Special-effects projectors take the audience through space into whirling galaxies and black holes. Shows change regularly. For daily shows, call 750-7141. There are shows on weekdays at 2 and on weekends at 1, 2, 3, and 4. (adults $2; ages 6–17 and seniors $1; under 6 by special permission). "Exploring the Skies of the Season," $1 for all, is shown at noon on weekends and holidays. Closed Thanksgiving and Christmas.

Laserium is a "cosmic" laser show in which colorful images pulsate, float, and dance to music against a background of stars. Shows are on Thursday through Sunday evenings. Call 750-7138 for titles, times, and prices. Not recommended for children under 6.

The whale-fountain courtyard leads to the Academy's **Steinhart Aquarium** swamp, inhabited by crocodiles and alligators. Thousands of fish, reptiles, and dolphins live in 243 colorful tanks, all low enough for children to see into easily. Sea horses, black-footed penguins, deadly stonefish, piranhas, and shellfish of all colors, shapes, and sizes live here. Upstairs, the *Fish Roundabout* puts you in the middle of a huge tank where fish swim quickly around you. The dolphins are fed every two hours; the penguins are fed at 11:30 and 4. For information, call 750-7145.

The Exploratorium

Palace of Fine Arts, Lyon Street. (415) 563-7337. Winter: Wednesday–Friday 1–5, weekends 10–5, Wednesday 7–9:30 p.m. Summer: Wednesday 11–9:30, Thursday and Friday 11–5, Saturday and Sunday 10–5. Closed Thanksgiving and Christmas. Adults $4.50 (good for 6 months); seniors $2.25 (lifetime pass); ages 6–17, $1 (6-month pass). Tape: 563-3200. Tactile Dome: 563-7272; $5 per person, by reservation. School groups and field trips. W.

This touchingthinkingpullingsplashingblinkingspinningopencloseamazing museum of science, art, and human perception contains 622 exhibits. It's the best example of learning-while-playing in California. Clap and a tree of lights blinks; blow a two-foot bubble; learn about light, language, patterns, vision, color, motion, and more. Laser beams, computers, holograms, stereophonic sound testers, and radio and TV sets are here to play with. Lively scientific exhibits demonstrate natural phenomena.

Across Marina Boulevard, at the end of the spit of land to the right of the St. Francis Yacht Club, is the **Wave Organ,** where you can sit and relax and listen to the activated voice of San Francisco Bay.

Young scientists face the challenge at the San Francisco Exploratorium.

*Aerodynamics fights back at the San
Francisco Exploratorium.*

Presidio Army Museum
*Funston and Lincoln boulevards, Presidio of San Francisco. (415) 561-4115.
Tuesday–Sunday 10–4. Groups by appointment: 921-8193.*

Founded by Spain's military forces in 1776, the Presidio has flown Spanish, Mexican, and American flags. Cannons, uniforms, swords, and Army
memorabilia tell the Presidio's 2,000-year history. Models and dioramas
originally constructed for the 1939 World's Fair at Treasure Island depict
the Presidio, the 1906 earthquake, and the 1915 Panama-Pacific Exposition. Outside are artillery pieces and two restored "earthquake cottages."

Fort Point National Historic Site (GGNRA)
*Foot of Marine Drive, on Presidio grounds, under the San Francisco end of
the Golden Gate Bridge. (415) 556-1693. Daily except holidays, 10–5.
Guided tours weekends and by appointment. Demonstrations on weekends at
1:30. Free.*

Nestled below the underpinnings of the Golden Gate Bridge, Fort Point, which was built during the Civil War, is the only brick coastal fort in the west, the guardian of San Francisco Bay. With the icy Pacific slamming into the retaining wall and the wind whistling around the point, this is one of the coldest spots in the City. Two special exhibits housed in the fort feature the contributions of women in the military, and the history and achievements of Black soldiers in the Army. Roam through the officer's and enlisted men's quarters; walk through the huge casements where once were mounted more than 100 huge cannon. Ask one of the park rangers dressed in Civil War uniforms to demonstrate how to load and fire a cannon. You may end up earning a cannoneer certificate. Check the schedule for special slide shows and a film telling how the Golden Gate Bridge was constructed.

California Palace of the Legion of Honor

Lincoln Park, off 34th Avenue and Clement. (415) 221-4841. Wednesday–Sunday 10–5. Adults $4, seniors $2, under 18 free. First Wednesday of the month free.

Children can explore Land's End and get a thrilling view of the Golden Gate Bridge from the ocean side after wandering through the impressive marble building, its rotating exhibitions, and the collection of fine French art and 20th-century printmakers. Maybe they'll recognize Rodin's *The Thinker* sitting in the courtyard.

The Cliff House (GGNRA)

"A drive to the 'Cliff' in the early morning. . . and a return to the city through the charming scenery of Golden Gate Park, tends to place man about as near to Elysian bliss as he may hope for in this world." B. E. Lloyd, 1876. A drive to and from the Cliff House can still place you in Elysian bliss. It's the best place in town to see the seals basking on Seal Rocks. A **Visitors Center** downstairs (556-8642) shows the Cliff House in its various incarnations throughout the years, along with rotating natural history displays. Here you can also find out about Farallon Island tours, the Whale Center (654-6621), and other adventures.

The crammed **Musée Mécanique** (386-1170; daily 11–7) houses over 100 coin-operated machines, old and new. Swiss music boxes, a mechanical carnival, a mechanical 1920s farm, old-time movies, and music

Children discover the hidden world of
insects at the San Francisco Zoo's Insect
Zoo.

machines sit alongside Star Trek, electronic games, and modern cartoons.
There are restaurants with great views upstairs.

San Francisco Zoo
Sloat Boulevard and Great Highway. (415) 661-2023. Daily 10–5. Adults
$4, seniors $1 for a quarterly pass, under 15 free with adult. Zoo Keys for
audiotour, $1.50. Additional charge for children's zoo, merry-go-round, and
zoomobile. Parties. Adopt-an-Animal programs. Summer junior volunteer
programs. Group tours. Strollers for rent. Picnic areas. W.

Have you an urge to pet a hissing cockroach? Ride a zebra train? Walk
through a tropical rain forest? San Francisco's state-of-the-art zoo is a natural setting for happy, healthy animals and youngsters who enjoy learning
about them. There are cassowary birds, white pheasants, black swans, kan-
garoos and koalas, Moulon and Barbary sheep, animals in the barnyard to
be petted, and big cats who are fed every day at 2 except Monday, because
they don't eat every day in the jungle, either. The Primate Discovery Center
is five stories of open atriums full of swinging monkeys and apes. On the
ground, the interactive exhibits provide for hands-on learning about the
animals in front of you. Musk Ox Meadow and the Tuxedo Junction Pen-
guin pool are extremely popular, as is the Insect Zoo, where you can even

Thumbs up! Children exploring the San Francisco Zoo's Primate Discovery Center opposable-thumb exhibit discover that they, too, are primates.

pet a tarantula. "Bone Carts" bring certain birds and animals to visitors for close-up learning. The 1921 Dentzel Carousel near the entrance is still as beautiful and dream-inspiring as ever.

Public Relations Tours

□ **KSFO and KYA.** 300 Broadway. (415) 398-5600. Free, by appointment. See news production, traffic continuity, and disc jockeys in action, with discussions on how each department operates.

Marin County

Marin County is a land of mountains and seashore north of the Golden Gate Bridge. Most of the places to go with children in Marin are natural wonders. You can drive to the top of Mt. Tamalpais and walk the trails overlooking miles of ocean, land, and city. You can explore the silent redwood groves of Muir Woods, then travel on to Stinson Beach or one of the lesser-known beaches for picnicking by the seaside, collecting driftwood, or wading in the icy sea. You can also spend hours fishing in the Marin lakes or hiking the beautiful Point Reyes National Seashore. And when you feel the need for civilization, you can head for Tiburon or Sausalito, where the children will be as enchanted as you by either of these bayside villages.

California Marine Mammal Center

Marin Headlands, Golden Gate National Recreation Area, Fort Cronkhite, near the batteries and bunkers on Rodeo Beach. Take the first exit off Hwy. 101 after Visa Point, and go through the tunnel. (415) 331-SEAL. Daily 10– 4. Tours and classes. W. Free.

Located in the Marin Headlands just across the Golden Gate Bridge, the California Marine Mammal Center is where we finally learned the difference between seals and sea lions. Seals are related to the weasel family. They don't have ears and do have whiskers. Sea lions are in the bear family. They do have ears—but no whiskers. The purpose of this center—which always needs volunteers—is to rescue and then release marine mammals stranded on the coast. Stranded pups are bottle-fed herring milkshakes. (Please remember that just because you see a sea otter on the beach it doesn't mean he needs rescuing. Don't touch unless you know what you're doing.) There are critters in cage-tanks to see, and informative illustrated panels to learn from. An exhibit center is in the works.

    The Pacific Energy and Resource Center next door explores the nature of energy and its resources, from sunshine to dirt, in kids' programs (Fort Cronkhite, Building 1055, 332-8200).

    The Point Bonita Lighthouse can also be reached through Fort Cronkhite. Although the light itself is way out on the rocks and worked by computer, you can reserve a tour, on weekends, at sunset, or during the full-moon walk, at 331-1540. Free.

Sausalito

After stopping for a moment to look back at the Golden Gate Bridge from Vista Point, spend a few hours in the Riviera by the Bay. Noted for years as an artists' colony, the village of Sausalito is now a mecca for tourists and young people. There are clothing and toy stores, ice cream parlors and coffeehouses, art galleries and restaurants for every age, taste, and budget.

*Visitors pose before the massive cross-
cut of a redwood log washed ashore
along the redwood coast in the mid-
1960s and now mounted in the viewing
area at the north end of Golden Gate
Bridge.*

The Sausalito Historical Museum, in the old City Hall on Litho Street, offers police and railroad memorabilia, period of costumes, and classic photos of the town (Wednesday and Saturday 1–5, Sunday 10–5; 332-1005, donation).

San Francisco Bay–Delta Model

2111 Bridgeway, Sausalito. (415) 332-3870. Tuesday–Saturday 9–4, summer weekends and holidays 10–6, and by appointment. W. Free.

The U. S. Army Corps of Engineers has constructed a huge hydraulic scale model of San Francisco Bay and the Sacramento-San Joaquin Delta. The model shows the action of the tides, the flow and currents of the water, and the mixing of sea water and fresh water. Guided tours take 1½ hours, but you can use the self-guided written information or the new tape-recorded audio program, which provides extensive information about the model and its operation. The model only operates when testing is scheduled, but there's so much to see—pictures, slides, models, etc., you'll be impressed.

Tiburon

Named *Punta de Tiburon,* or Shark Point, by Spanish settlers, Tiburon is a quiet, one-street bayside village, a nice place to spend a sunny afternoon. Having lunch, indoors or out, while enjoying the view of the city from one of the restaurants on the bay can be heaven. Nautical shops, a Swedish bakery, and the bookstore are all fun to browse through. Our favorite restaurant is right next to the ferry landing: **Guaymas** (5 Main Street, 435-6300), for the kind of grilled fish and fowl you'd have in a seaside Mexican village. Hardy walkers can head up the hill to the **Landmark Society Museum in Old St. Hilary's Church** (Sunday and Wednesday 1–4, April–September, and by appointment; (415) 435-1853; 50¢) to see a changing art exhibition and specimens of local plants that grow nowhere else in the world. The Landmark Society also operates the new **China Cabin Museum** on the cove in nearby Belvedere. The 20-by-40-foot cabin, from the S.S. *China Cabin,* a side-wheel steamer, looks exactly as it did when it left New York for San Francisco in June 1867, on its first voyage (Wednesday and Sunday 1–4; 435-1853; free). You can go to Tiburon by bus, ferry, or car (take Highway 101 to the Tiburon exit).

Richardson Bay Audubon Center

376 Greenwood Beach Road, Tiburon, (415) 388-2525, Wednesday–Sunday 9–5. Lyford House: Sunday 1–4, October–May. $1. Public nature walks on Sundays at 9 and 1.

Richardson Bay Audubon Center and Sanctuary provides a habitat for wildlife and is an environmental education center, a "window on the bay." Youngsters can explore the sea life and observe birds on nature trails. Pro-

Birdwatchers love tromping through the marsh grass at Richardson Bay Wildlife Sanctuary. The beautiful Victorian in the background is the Lyford House.

grams, films, and classes help make visitors aware of the wonders around them. The focal point of the center is the yellow and white Victorian mansion, Lyford House, with period furnishings.

Muir Woods National Monument

Off Highway 1, on Muir Woods Road. (415) 388-2595. 8 a.m. to sunset. Free. W.

This lovely forest of giant coast redwoods, some more than 200 feet high, is a breathtaking way to start the day. Among these magnificent trees, you'll encounter many other species of plant life, as well as an occasional black-tailed deer and, in summer, young salmon swimming through Redwood Creek. Naturalist John Muir wrote, "This is the best tree lover's monument that could be found in all the forests of the world." A snack bar, gift shop, and ranger's station are near the park entrance. There are several self-guided trails, including one in Braille. Junior ranger packs are offered free to young naturalists.

At Muir Woods National Monument, giant coastal redwoods tower over visitors along trails of spectacular beauty.

Angel Island State Park

For tour information call the Angel Island Association at (415) 435-3522. For ferry schedules from San Francisco, call 546-2815. Ferry from Tiburon daily in summer, and on weekends or by arrangement in winter. Call 435-2131. Adults $4, children $3, bikes 50¢. Ranger station: 435-1915. Classes, tours, and groups, including disabled: 435-3522.

Angel Island was the Ellis Island of the Pacific for Asian immigrants. Today, it's a wonderful place to spend the day (or stay overnight; call 916-323-2988 for reservations). Most visitors ride the ferries to Ayala Cove, where lawn, beach, and barbecue pits beckon. The Visitors Center has interpretive nature and history displays, with a 35-minute video. Open weekends, April through October; free. Camp Reynolds, Fort McDowell, and the Barracks Museum at the Immigration Station are staffed by docents who'll give tours and tell stories.

Angel Island picnics are fun for all ages.

Marin County Historical Society Museum
1125 B Street, Boyd Park, San Rafael (off Third). (415) 454-8538. Wednesday–Sunday 1–4. Free.

Designed to "stir the imagination and bring back panoramas of the past," this overstuffed museum displays original Mexican land grants and mementos of the Miwoks, Mexicans, and pioneers who settled Marin. Lillie Coit's shoes, an early San Quentin oil lamp, and the military collection are notable. A favorite with youngsters is the huge tallow kettle at the entrance. Once used for boiling elk tallow for candles and soap at the *Rancho Olompali,* the area's original farm, the kettle was also used as a stew pot for the military during the Bear Flag War.

Just down the block is the **Mission San Rafael Archangel** (1104 Fifth Avenue; (415) 454-8141; 11–4 daily, from 10 on Sunday, free). Inside the small chapel, the six flags under which the mission has served still fly: Spain, Mexico, the California Republic, the United States of 1850, the Vatican, and the United States of America.

The Wildlife Center
76 Albert Park Lane, off B Street, San Rafael. (415) 54-6961. Tuesday–Saturday 10–4. Donation. W.

This small wildlife rehabilitation and nature education center cares for and releases back into the wilderness over 4,000 birds and animals a year. Volunteers are needed! The gist of the touch-and-guess boxes and other interactive exhibits is to show how wild animals interact among themselves and with humans. A little zoo outside exhibits a golden eagle, a black bear, owls, and other animals that can no longer fend for themselves.

Bay Area Discovery Museum
428 Town Center, in the shopping center, off Highway 101, Corte Madera. (415) 927-4722. Wednesday–Sunday 11–5, $1 per person. First Thursday of the month, 5–8, free.

Parents and kids come here to play and end up learning, sometimes about each other. As one reviewer wrote: "The educational element goes down like vitamin D in an ice cream cone." Here you can design a house, sail on a boat, walk through an underwater adventure tunnel, draw pictures, and be an actor on stage, in costume. The museum hopes to move to more permanent quarters in Fort Baker soon.

Audubon Canyon Ranch
Highway 1, 3 miles north of Stinson Beach. (415) 868-9244. Weekends and holidays 10–4, mid-March to mid-July and by appointment. Free (donations welcome). W.

This 1,000-acre wildlife sanctuary bordering on the Bolinas Lagoon is a peaceful spot to view birds "at home." From a hilltop, you can watch the nesting activities of the great blue heron and the great egret. The ranch's pond, stream, and canyon are a living demonstration of the region's ecology, the delicate balance between plant and animal life and their environment. The display hall shows local fauna and flora and includes information on the San Andreas fault. Picnic areas.

Point Reyes National Seashore
Highway 1, Olema. (415) 663-1092. Open 8 to sundown daily. Free.

When Sir Francis Drake landed here in 1579, he wrote of a "Faire & Good Baye, with a good wind to enter the same." Today's visitors will agree. The beauty of the cliffs, the surf—swimmable in some places—the tidepools, lowlands, and forest meadows make you wonder why he went back to England. You can follow nature trails, bird-watch, backpack, picnic, rent horses, and camp. We like Drake's Bay best, and before we set out, we call the ranger's office there (669-1250) to check the weather. The cafe is nicely protected and even serves fresh oysters.

Start your visit at the *Bear Valley Visitors Center* (open 8–5 on weekends, from 9 on weekdays). You can get maps with suggested itineraries and all the information you may need while the kids watch a movie or slide show or explore the beautifully designed walk-through diorama of the world of Point Reyes. Our favorite of the interactive exhibits is a large log attached to a handle. When you press down, the log lifts up to show all the creepy-crawlies living underneath. Classes and special programs are listed on the schedule.

From Bear Valley, you can walk to the Morgan Horse Ranch (9–4:30 daily; 663-1763) along the Earthquake Trail, or to *Kule Loklo*, the replica of a Coastal Miwok village. A reconstructed granary, sunshade, sweat house, and *Kotcas,* "the place where real people live," have been built with authentic materials by volunteers. On weekends there are demonstrations on skills like hunting, sewing, weaving, and preparing acorn mush. (sunrise to sunset; interpretive programs on request; 663-1092).

The Ken Patrick Visitors Center at Drake's Beach has displays on the Gulf of the Farallones National Marine Sanctuary, various intertidal creatures found within the seashore, and lots of interesting seashells to touch. (10–5 weekends and holidays; 669-1250).

The Point Reyes Lighthouse is open, Thursday through Monday from 10 to 4:30, with regular tours. You have to walk down a narrow path to get there, because the light was meant to shine *below* the fog line on Marin's rocky coast. Since whale-watching is increasingly popular, and the best place around is the lighthouse, the park supplies free weekend shuttle bus service from Drake's Beach to the Point Reyes Lighthouse (669-1534).

Tomales Bay State Park (open daily 8–8 in summer, until 6 in winter; 669-1140; $2 per car) has beaches for swimming and picnic facilities. The tidepools, rocky pockets that retain seawater when the tide goes out, pro-

*A hungry young crab lover seems puzzled
by the empty crab traps at Tomales Bay.*

vide endless hours of fascination—as long as you watch very quietly as the tidepool's occupants move through their daily routines. Seaweeds, anemones, barnacles, jellyfish, sand dollars, tiny fish, and flowery algae can hide if they want to!

Hang Gliders West
Dillon Beach Flying School, 20A Pamaron Way, Novato. (415) 883-3494.

The perfect present for the youngster who has everything would be a day of hang gliding over the soft dunes at Dillon Beach. Flights are low and slow, with an emphasis on safety. You can expect at least two flights on your first lesson. Teaching programs vary in time and cost, so call to choose.

Johnson's Drake's Bay Oysters
Sir Francis Drake Boulevard, on the way to Drake's Bay in Point Reyes National Seashore. (415) 669-1149. 8–4:30 daily.

Follow the crushed oyster-shell driveway to the "farm" to see how oysters are raised—and buy a small succulent sample to taste in the sea air. Did you know that it takes 18 months for an oyster to grow?

Up Highway One, on Tomales Bay, is the *Tomales Bay Oyster Company,* (415) 663-1242. Usually open Friday through Sunday from 9 to 5 for sales (but no on the spot tasting), the newly refurbished oyster company displays the many "fields" of stakes spread out in the bay, each staking holding about 100 oysters. Different holding tanks hold seed, juvenile, and harvest-size oysters. Bay mussels are also grown on the farm. Kids love the bags of "empties."

Marin Museum of the American Indian
2200 Novato Boulevard, Miwok Park, Novato. (415) 897-4064. Tuesday–Saturday 10–4, Sunday 12–4; docent tour Sunday at 1:30. Free.

The permanent exhibit, "Coast Miwok Indians: The First People of Marin," explores local history and the interaction of early inhabitants with the natural environment of Marin County. A Touch Table invites visitors to participate in a hands-on experience. Temporary exhibits focus on other aspects of Indian cultures of the western United states. Classes, lectures, and films are offered, so call for schedules. The California Native Plant Garden and surrounding park are super for nature walks and picnics.

In downtown Novato, the *Novato History Museum*, in the home of the town's first postmaster, focuses on the history of Hamilton Air Force Base (815 Delong Avenue; 897-1164; Tuesday–Saturday 10–4; free).

The East Bay: Alameda and Contra Costa Counties

The East Bay, ranging along the east shore of San Francisco Bay, is dotted with public parks and streams and crowned by Mt. Diablo. The places of interest in this area are some distance from each other, so plan ahead and call for up-to-the-minute times and prices. Boaters, fishermen, picknickers, hikers, and nature lovers of all ages will find special places to visit here.

Navy, Marine Corps, Coast Guard Museum
Building 1, Treasure Island, off the Bay Bridge. (415) 765-6182. 10–3:30 daily. W. Groups by appointment. Free.

Drive past one of the great views of San Francisco up to an art deco masterpiece built for the 1939 World's Fair and enter a large, airy collection of naval memories. The activities of the Navy, Marine Corps, and Coast Guard in Pacific waters from before the Civil War to tomorrow's space ventures are well presented. The Farallon Islands Lighthouse lens, a 1919 diver's suit, ship models, World's Fair mementos, and Pearl Harbor Day photos are on display, towered over by Lowell Nesbitt's vast mural of the past, present, and future of American services in the Pacific.

TJ's Gingerbread House
741 Fifth Street, Oakland. Take the Broadway exit on route 880. (415) 444-7373. Lunch: Tuesday–Saturday 12 and 1:30. Dinner: Tuesday–Thursday 6 and 8; Friday 6, 8, and 10; Saturday 4, 6, 8, and 10. Gazebo downstairs (W) available for parties.

Hansel and Gretel's wicked witch would be envious of this restaurant, which looks good enough to eat. In a tiny shop downstairs, you'll find gingerbread cookies, puppets, dolls, T-shirts, soaps, tea—even gingerbread bubble bath. Upstairs, in a fantasy land of dolls, T.J. Robinson serves copi-

*T. J.'s Gingergread House is delicious,
inside and out.*

ous Cajun-Creole lunches and dinners to diners who order their main
course when they make their reservations. Prices range from $16 for Bayou
Spiced-Baked Catfish and "Spoon" Jambalaya, and up. We can vouch for
the whiskey-stuffed lobster, the rabbit piquante, the smoked prime rib, the
cherry duck, and the Pick-Your-Heart-Out-Chicken. Each meal comes with
fruit salad, Cajun "come-back" dirty rice, vegetables, "sassy" corn bread, a
beverage, and an ice cream-with-gingerbread cookie. For a nominal price,
children can just order their own fruit salad, rice, and dessert.

East Bay Negro Historical Society
*Golden Gate Library, 5606 San Pablo Avenue, Oakland. (415) 658-3158.
Tuesday 12:30–7, Wednesday–Friday 12:30–5:30, and by appointment.
Free.*

California's Black Americans and their history is the theme of this lovingly
put-together collection, which focuses on local families and also recalls
Black American athletes, musicians, scientists, politicians, gold miners,
cowboys, farmers, and doctors. Pio Pico, an early governor of California;
Black mountaineer James Beckworth; "Mammy" Pleasant; William A. Lei-

desdorff, who built one of San Francisco's first hotels and launched the first steamer in San Francisco Bay; and Colonel Allensworth, a Black Army chaplain who founded one of the state's first Black communities, are some of the people youngsters will "meet" here.

Dunsmuir House and Garden

2960 Peralta Oaks Court, 106 Avenue exit on Highway 580. (415) 562-0328. April–September, Sunday and Wednesday 12–4. Christmas display from Thanksgiving through December. House tour: adults $3, children and seniors $2. Garden tour: $1.

This 37-room Colonial Revival mansion is set in a 40-acre estate in the East Oakland foothills. A visit will provide an enlightening sense of another way of life through architecture, photos, and garden strolls. Dunsmuir is the site of movies, weddings, and seasonal events.

The Oakland Museum

1000 Oak Street, Oakland. (415) 273-3401. Information (415) 834-2413. Wednesday–Saturday 10–5, Sunday 12–7. Closed holidays. W. Free.

The Oakland Museum is three first-rate museums in one: California art, California history, and California natural sciences. You can always be sure of finding an afternoon's worth of interesting things for children of all ages.

One level concentrates on art from the days of the Spanish explorers to the present. Panoramic views of San Francisco and Yosemite, cityscapes and landscapes, and contemporary jewelry, ceramics, photos, paintings, and sculpture create a historic continuity in the visual arts.

The natural sciences gallery takes you across the nine zones of California, from the coast to the snow-capped Sierras, with their ancient bristlecone pines. Dioramas of mammals, birds, rodents, and snakes in their native habitats provide fascinating replicas of the real thing.

Kids will like the California history level best of all. Begin with the Native Californians, the many Indian tribes, and walk through the superbly furnished "rooms" of the state's history, from the Spanish explorers and *Californios,* to the gold miners and cowboys, to the pioneers, Victorian San Franciscans, to the "California Dream," from *Beach Party* to *American Graffiti* and the Summer of Love.

We always head for the 1890s shiny red fire pumper and the pioneer kitchen with the chair outside the glass—to bring the visitor into the pic-

**Victorian era children live again in the
history section of the Oakland Museum.**

ture. Concerts, films, and special exhibits are scheduled regularly, and the
snack bar is open until 4, Wednesday through Saturday and until 5 on
Sunday; the restaurant is open from 11–3, Wednesday through Friday.

Paramount Theater

2025 Broadway, Oakland; Highway 880 to Downtown exit. (415) 893-2300. Tours first and third Saturday of the month at 10 a.m. $1 per person. Children under 10 not encouraged. By appointment.

The Paramount, which has programs of interest to children, is the best example of Art Deco architecture on the West Coast. Parquet floors, a gold ceiling teeming with sculptured life, and elegant embellishments almost compete with what's on stage.

The Camron-Stanford House

1418 Lakeside Drive, Oakland. (415) 836-1976. Tours Wednesday 11–4 and Sunday 1–5, and by appointment. Free.

This 1876 Italianate-style Victorian, once the Oakland Museum, provides a look at Oakland history since the days of the horse cars and gas lighting. Four rooms are furnished to show the local style of the Victorian era. Multi-media shows, special exhibits, and engaging curators add to the young visitor's enjoyment.

Lakeside Park

Off Grand Avenue, Lake Merritt, Oakland.

A narrow strip of grass around Lake Merritt creates a peaceful oasis in the center of a busy city. In the Kiwanis Kiddie Korner, children can slide down an octopus or swing on a sea horse. **The Rotary Natural Science Center** offers an educational exhibit of native reptiles, mammals, and birds as well as an observation beehive. (415-273-3090; Tuesday–Sunday 10–5, Monday 12–5; free).

   Lake Merritt is the oldest wildlife refuge in the United States for free-flying waterfowl, which includes an occasional pelican. Sailboats, houseboats, and paddleboats are available for renting. The **Merritt Queen**, a replica of a Mississippi riverboat, takes half-hour tours of the lake on weekends and in summer ($1 for adults, 50¢ for children and seniors).

Children's Fairyland

Lakeside Park, Lake Merritt, Oakland. (415) 452-2259. Wednesday–Sunday 10–4:30 in spring and fall and on winter weekends and school holidays; daily 10–5:30 in summer. Adults $2, children $1.

Duck through the Old Woman's Shoe to meet Alice, the Chesire Cat, and the Cowardly Lion. Then slide down a dragon's back or sail on a pea-green boat with the Owl and the Pussycat. Pinocchio, Willie the Whale, slides, mazes, rides, and enchanted bowers come to life. All the characters in Fairyland are here to make children smile, and a magic key unlocks their stories ($1). The Wonder-Go-Round and Magic Web Ferris wheel are nominally priced; puppet shows are free.

Knowland Park, Oakland Zoo

9777 Golf Links Road, Oakland, at 98th Avenue off Highway 580. (415) 632-9525. Park admission $2 per car. Zoo: Adults $2; 2–14 and over 60, $1. Group discounts. Rides 50¢ and $1. W.

This beautifully arranged zoo is one of the nicest in the state. Glide over the African Veldt and up into the hills on the 1,250-foot Skyfari Ride or ride a miniature train for a breathtaking view of the bay. Over 330 animals from around the world make their home in 525 acres of rolling green parkland. The Children's Petting Zoo will make tots' barnyard tales come alive. Picnic, barbecue, and playground facilities are located throughout the park.

Chabot Observatory and Planetarium

4917 Mountain Boulevard, near MacArthur Freeway and Warren Boulevard, Oakland. (415) 531-4560. Friday and Saturday 7:30 p.m. Adults $1.50, children 50¢. Reservations advised. The Chabot Science Center is open irregularly, 6 or 7 days a week, so call ahead.

The changing two-hour show here includes a movie, science demonstrations, a planetarium program, and observation of the heavens through a large telescope. A recent show presented an exciting space voyage. Youngsters learn how astronomers explore the universe. Locating the Big and Little Dippers during the planetarium show is always a popular part of the program.

University Art Museum
2626 Bancroft Way, Berkeley. (415) 642-1207. Wednesday–Sunday 11–5. Ages 18–64, $3; ages 6–17 and over 65, $2. Free admission Thursday between 11 and 12. Snack bar. W.

Berkeley's museum is a natural for children, not so much for the art as for the building itself. Its unique multileveled concrete-slab construction enables a young visitor to see its spacious interiors from any of the many corners and balconies. The outdoor sculpture garden is fun and strikes a chord with young people. The Pacific Film Archive, located in the museum, shows classical, international, and children's films. Call (415) 642-1412 for schedules.

This two year old is almost ready to ride Ruthie, a three-year-old miniature horse at the Oakland Zoo.

Children at the Oakland Zoo pet and feed friendly animals.

McCallum's Famous Ice Cream

1825 Solano, Berkeley. (415) 525-3510. Monday–Thursday 8 a.m. to 11 p.m., Friday until midnight, Saturday 10 a.m.–midnight, Sunday 11–11. W.

McCallum's has been around a long time. It may need some freshening up, but the ice cream maker is still right on target with new flavors. Half the store is for cones and take-home orders. The other half is for on-the-spot gluttony: hot fudge sundaes served with a pitcher of hot sauce on the side, or a tall shake in a glass lined with fudge, or a "Nightmare" for a group effort.

Lawrence Hall of Science

Centennial Drive, University of California, Berkeley. Up Hearst to the top of the University to Gayley Road, to Rim Way, to Centennial, just south of Grizzly Peak Boulevard. (415) 642-5132. Monday–Saturday 10–4:30, Sunday noon–5. Adults $3.50; students, seniors, and children $2.50. W. Galaxy Snack Bar.

There are young scientists who'd rather spend a day here than anywhere else in the world. The Hall features an outstanding variety of exhibits, science workshops, tests of your mathematical and logical ability, tests of knowledge, computers to play with, visual oddities, and a hundred different things to tantalize and amuse. Tots love the growling apatosaurus. Others are fascinated by the laser exhibit. Ocean Voyaging in Polynesia sweeps others away. The Biology Lab is the place to investigate the world of living things; the Wizard's Lab is for super experiments (both, weekends 1:30–4:30, daily in summer). Holt Planetarium shows, the Science Discovery Theater, films, and special events offer ever-changing inducements to learning. The replica of the *Challenger* shuttlecraft on the grounds is also a challenge to explorers.

Lowie Museum of Anthropology

Kroeber Hall, Bancroft Way at College Avenue, University of California, Berkeley. (415) 643-7648. Monday, Tuesday, Thursday, Friday 10–4:30; weekends 12–4:30. Donation. Free admission on Thursday.

Word games with a computer at the Lawrence Hall of Science.

The museum's rotating exhibits are developed from its vast holdings of eth-nographic, archaeological, and archival materials. A visit will help children understand other peoples' worlds, past and present. A special presentation on Ishi, the last Yahi Indian, is offered during the summer months in the Teaching Exhibits gallery. The museum also features lectures, movies, and slide presentations.

The Campanile

Sather Tower, University of California. (415) 642-5215. Daily 10–4:15. 50¢

From the top of this tower, you can see San Francisco, Alcatraz, Mt. Tamal-pais, the Golden Gate and Bay bridges, and the entire campus. Above you, 61 bronze bells, the largest weighing 10,000 pounds, ring out melodies three times a day. You can see them being played.

Hall of Health

2001 Dwight Way, Berkeley. (415) 549-1564. Monday, Wednesday, Friday 10–3; Tuesday and Thursday until 4. Groups by appointment. Drop-in visits encouraged. Free.

"Your body is yours for life . . . take care of it yourself" is the motto here. The Hall of Health encourages visitors to interact with games, displays, and equipment so they can learn with all of their senses. They can ride and ex-ercycle, test their knowledge of nutrition, see how babies are born, and study the circulatory system in films and in person.

Tilden Regional Park

Canon Drive off Grizzly Peak Boulevard, Berkeley. (415) 525-2233. Nomi-nal prices for rides, with varying times depending on the season. The Little Farm is open daily, 8:30–5. Free.

Tilden Park has a pony ride, a historic merry-go-round, and a miniature train. The native California botanical gardens, an Environmental Educa-tional Center, wooded hiking trails, and swimming in Lake Anza are also popular. But the chief attraction for youngsters is the Little Farm in the Na-ture Area. Here they can meet barnyard animals like sheep, goats, cows, pigs, chickens, geese, rabbits, and a sociable donkey.

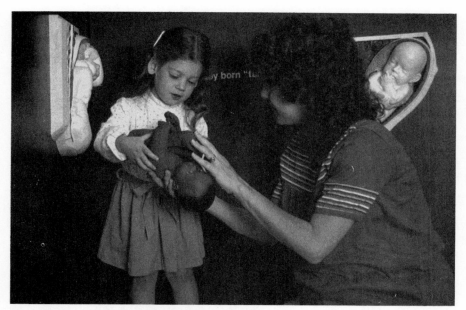

**Using the birth exhibit models in the Hall
of Health helps prepare this little girl for
her role as big sister.**

McConaghy Estate

*18701 Hesperian Boulevard, Hayward. Off Highway 17 between Hacienda
and A streets. (415) 276-3010. Thursday–Sunday 1–4, and by appointment.
(415) 278-0198. Adults $2; seniors $1.50; children 6–12, 50¢. Classes $5.
Special Christmas program.*

This elegant 1886 farmhouse is so completely furnished it looks as if the
family still lives there. One bedroom is filled with toys, games, books, and
clothes used by a turn-of-the-century child. The kitchen displays an ice-
box, a wood stove, and a water pump. The dining room is lavishly decorated for each holiday. A tank house and a buggy-filled carriage house
adjoin the house, handily located next to Kennedy Park with its picnic tables, merry-go-round, and train.

The nearby **Meek Estate** is also open for tours, by appointment. This
1869 Victorian Italian villa still boasts many of the original furnishings.
Youngsters will be intrigued by the meat cellar in the basement, by the old
carriage house—now a little theater—and by the tank house, which provided the water for the estate (grounds open to the public for picnics and

A happy four year old explores the old-fashioned toys at the McConaghy House nursery.

barbecues; tot play area; Hampton and Boston roads, Hayward; 415-581-6331).

Hayward Area Historical Society Museum
22701 Main Street at C, Hayward. (415) 581-0223. Monday–Friday 11–4, Saturday 12–4. Closed holidays. Free.

The large brick 1927 post office is now a lovingly presented album of Hayward area history. Cameras, dolls, scrapbooks full of high school pictures, tax records, family albums, a 1923 fire engine, an 1820s hand-drawn fire pumper that was shipped around the Horn to San Francisco in 1849, a 1912 Oakland automobile, a turn-of-the-century washing machine, a pump organ, and a 1930's post office present an engaging glimpse of the lifestyle of the past. The old phonograph can be wound up and played for youngsters, and the old stereopitcon may be looked into. Exhibits change three times a year to keep visitors returning. A favorite is the holiday collection of toys, dolls, Christmas ornaments, lights, and cards.

Sulphur Creek Nature Center
1801 D Street, Hayward. (415) 881-6747. Tuesday–Sunday 10–5, W. Free.

Sulphur Creek park is a charming spot in which to introduce children to wildlife native to Northern California. Coyotes, raccoons, opossums, skunks, hawks, owls, song and garden birds, and a variety of reptiles, amphibians, and invertebrates are displayed in naturalistic habitats. There are changing exhibits and a wildlife garden. Nature study classes, wildlife rehabilitation, and volunteer opportunities are available.

Hayward Shoreline Interpretive Center
4901 Breakwater Avenue, Hayward. (415) 881-6751. Tuesday–Sunday 10–5. Free.

Located on the Hayward shore of San Francisco Bay, this center is the hub of an 1,800-acre marshland park. You can explore marine life in a hands-on Wet Lab, search for animal life under the microscope, see an exhibit on birds of the shoreline area, check out a free Family Discovery Pack or binoculars, or hike on eight miles of trails. Public programs on weekends.

Mission San Jose
43300 Mission Boulevard, Fremont. (415) 657-1797. Daily 10–5. Closed holidays. W. Donation.

Founded in 1797, Mission San Jose holds an exciting place in California history. A highlight of the museum tour is an exhibit on the Ohlone, the native people of the Bay Area. Father Duran, who arrived in 1806, taught some of the 2,000 Ohlone neophytes to play the original mission bells and musical instruments now on display. Original Mission vestments, the original baptismal font, a pioneer cradle, and the sanctus bells are housed in the adobe living quarters of the mission padres. The mission church has been carefully reconstructed from hand-hewn beams and more than 180,000 adobe bricks.

San Francisco Bay Natural Wildlife Refuge
Highway 84 near Dumbarton Bridge toll plaza, at the west end of Thornton Avenue, Fremont. (415) 792-3178. Daily 10–5. Free. Special weekend programs.

Photographic exhibitions on special environmental programs, nature study walks, slide and film programs, and self-guided walks through the salt marsh and diked ponds at Newark Slough help introduce youngsters to the world around them.

Wind Farms of Altamont Pass
Interstate 580, Greenville Road and Mountain House Road exits, east of Livermore.

On windy days you can often hear them before you see them—the more than 7,500 giant wind turbines, perched on towers, on either side of Interstate 580. They comprise the world's largest "wind farm" producing electricity from the wind. A seven-mile drive just north of and paralleling I-580, begun either from Greenville or Mountain House roads, tours you through the heart of the wind farms.

Livermore History Center
2155 Third Street, Livermore. (415) 449-9927. Wednesday–Sunday 11:30–4. Free.

This exhibit of the history of the Livermore Valley from prehistoric times to the present is housed in the old Carnegie Library. Pictures, maps, artifacts, and mementos from local families, businesses, and groups are on display. A 19th-century drugstore exhibit has been installed. The museum members are currently working on the restoration of the historical Duarte Garage/Lincoln Highway Museum in Livermore at North L Street and Portola. Early-day fire trucks, wagons, and other apparatus can be viewed by appointment.

Ravenswood, the Victorian-era home and gardens of San Francisco's "Blind Boss" Christopher Buckley, is occasionally open to the public (on Arroy Road; call 447-7300 for an appointment). Visitor will see cloisonné chandeliers, an ornate billiard table, clothing, pictures, and mementos of the Buckley family.

Lawrence Livermore National Laboratory
Visitors Center: Greenville Road, between East Avenue and Highway 580, Livermore. (415) 422-9797. Monday–Friday 9–4:30, weekends 12–5. Closed holidays. Computer Museum: 1401 Almond Avenue, off East Avenue a

block from LLNL. (415) 423-7015. Tuesday and Thursday 10–5, and by appointment. Picnic areas. W. Free.

"How does a computer talk?" "What's a *Star Wars* weapon?" "Can scientists make something as hot as the sun?" The answers to these and many other intriguing questions about science can be found at Lawrence Livermore National Laboratory's Visitors Center. Hands-on exhibits, displays, films, audiotapes, and a multimedia show explain the laboratory's mission. Visitors will learn about lasers, fusion energy, biomedical and environmental research, energy, and resources.

The Laboratory has just opened a **Computer Museum**, which displays photographs, computer parts, and hardware and software that can actually be used. Computers are explored from the ancient past (1953) to the present.

Amador-Livermore Valley Museum
603 Main street, Pleasanton. (415) 462-2766. Wednesday–Friday 11–4, Saturday and Sunday 1–4. Free. W.

Housed in the 1914 Town Hall, this museum features platform exhibits of yesteryear, including a blacksmith shop and a general store. Rotating exhibits explore the Tri-Valley area's history from fossil remains to the present. The Museum Art Gallery exhibitions rotate regularly and feature artists in all media.

Richmond Museum
400 Nevin Avenue, Richmond. (415) 235-7387. Thursday–Sunday 1–4, except holiday weekends, and by appointment. Free.

Richmond residents from the days of the Native Americans up to 1945 are portrayed in the history gallery of this bright new museum through dioramas and panel displays. Old-time vehicles such as a peddler's wagon and an old fire engine are on the site. Kids will also enjoy the re-creations of rooms and old stores, as well as the changing exhibits, which range from antique toys to African artifacts to fishermen on the bay.

Diablo Valley College Museum and Planetarium
321 Golf Club Road, off Willow Pass Road from Highway 680, Pleasant Hill. (415) 684-1230. Hours change each semester. Groups by appointment. Donation.

In this museum youngsters can see a seismograph working, a Foucault pendulum swinging, and changing oceanography and anthropological exhibits on Native Americans. Local animals, especially nocturnal moles, weasels, and owls, are fun to see too, as are the star shows. Planetarium shows.

The Lindsay Museum
1901 First Avenue, Larkey Park (Highway 680 to Main to Buena Vista to First), Walnut Creek. (415) 935-1978. Wednesday–Sunday 1–5 during school time, Wednesday–Sunday 11–5 in summer. W. Free.

A collection of native wild animals, aquariums of native fish and amphibians, and a collection of rocks, fossils, and Indian artifacts are the main features of this sparkling small museum, best known for its Wildlife Rehabilitation Program, which cares for injured and orphaned wild animals and birds. Foxes, owls, hawks, a raccoon, a vulture, a brush rabbit, and a king snake are a few of the animals on display. The Pet Library usually has rabbits, rats, hamsters, and guinea pigs on hand. Talks, walks, classes, and safaris are offered by this learning center for people interested in the natural sciences. Volunteers of all ages are always needed in the Wildlife Department, which cares for about 7,500 hurt animals a year.

History buffs will also want to visit **Shadelands Ranch Historical Museum**, a few blocks away, a restored home with farm implements in back, at 2660 Ygnacio Valley Road, Walnut Creek (415-935-7871; Wednesday 11:30–4, Sunday 1–4; $2 for adults).

Eugene O'Neill National Historic Site
Tours by reservation only, at 10 a.m. and 1:30 p.m., when an 11-passenger van picks up visitors in the Clock Tower parking lot behind Railroad and Diablo roads off Interstate 680. Call (415) 838-0249.

Tao House, where Eugene O'Neill wrote some of his greatest plays, is now a museum run by the National Park Service. Although many of the rooms are bare, the beauty of the surrounding Las Trampas hills echoes the solace O'Neill found here.

The Alvarado Adobe and Blume House Museum
1 Alvarado Square, at the intersection of San Pablo Avenue and Church Lane, San Pablo. Off Highway 80. 4202 Alhambra Avenue, Martinez, CA 94553. (415) 236-7373. Weekends 1–5, and by appointment. Donation.

The Alvarado Adobe has been precisely reconstructed on its original site. The owner, Juan Bautista Alvarado, husband of Martina Castro, was the Mexican governor of California in 1840 and lived here until 1882. The house itself was built in the early 1840s by the Castro family and is furnished in a mix of Rancho and Early California styles. Visitors can see showcases of artifacts found in local Indian mounds; *cascarone* (painted eggshells filled with confetti or cologne, which were tossed at fellow party goes); an Indian shell game; and samples of *amole,* the soap plant, which was roasted and eaten, boiled for glue, pounded into a paste that stupefied fish when thrown into a stream, dried to stuff mattresses and used for twine, shampoo, and soap.

The Blume Museum is a 1907 farmhouse now refurnished to look as it did then, with oak furniture, early plumbing fixtures, and an iron stove in the kitchen.

Castro Point Railway
Point Molato Road at the Richmond end of Richmond-San Rafael Bridge. (415) 234-6473. 11–4. Donation.

On the first Sunday of each month, the Pacific Locomotive Association opens its doors to the public. The 1½ miles of track and the collection of cabooses, coaches, and open cars have been restored by volunteers.

Crockett Historical Museum
900 Loring Avenue, Crockett. On the water's edge in the old railroad depot. Wednesday and Saturday 10–3. Free.

Pictures, medals, trophies, a stocked kitchen, model ships, and memorabilia of the oil fields of the thirties are just part of this admirable collection.

Muriel's Doll House Museum

33 Canyon Lake Drive, Port Costa. Highway 80 to Port Costa Exit. (415) 787-2820. Daily except Monday 10–7, and by appointment. Adults $1, children 25¢.

Muriel's is heaven for doll lovers. Muriel herself greets you at the door and introduces you to her huge and ever-increasing collection of dolls and dollhouses. There are china, bisque, parian, wood, wax, apple, tin, celluloid, papier-mâché, cornhusk, rag, and fashion dolls reflecting the customs and costumes of their eras. There are Indian dolls, Eskimo dolls, Amish dolls, Black dolls, Shirley Temples, John Muir, and Queen Elizabeth—even Helen Hayes starring as Sarah Winchester. Anna and the King of Siam dance on. Miniature scenes and the replica of Muriel's childhood Victorian home in Ohio are engrossing. Muriel enjoys sharing stories about the dolls and makes visits most enjoyable.

Benicia Capitol State Historic Park

First & G Streets, Benicia (707) 745-3385. Daily 10–5, except Tuesday and Wednesday in winter. Adults, $1 ages 6–19, 50¢

Benicia was the first capital of California, and it still looks like it did in 1853. The exhibit rooms portray a bit of California history—right down to the whale-oil lamps, quill pens, shiny brass cuspidors, and varied headgear on all the desks. The Senate is on the first floor, the Assembly on the second. Interactive displays also bring the past to life.

The **Fisher-Hanlon House** next door is also part of the State Historic Park complex. This fine old Federal-style house, its creamery and its carriage house, complete with buggy and cart, horses and manure, has been lovingly restored by volunteers. This is a proper, upper-class merchant's home of the 1880s, and the Hanlon sisters lived in it until they gave it to the state in the last decade.

Don't forget to go across town to the **Camel Barns** in the Arsenal on Camel Road off Park. These large sandstone warehouses now serve as nicely designed art galleries and a historical museum, but they actually housed 35 Army camels from 1856 to 1864. Weekends, 1–4, also Friday in summer. Tours by appointment (donation requested).

Benicia is a cosy little town on the Bay, a mecca for antique collectors.

John Muir National Historic Site

4202 Alhambra Avenue, Martinez, off John Muir Parkway. (415) 228-8860. The house is open for self-guided tours, 8:30–4:30 daily. Guided tours and Environmental Living Programs by reservation. Donation.

"I hold dearly cherished memories about it [the house] and fine garden grounds full of trees and bushes and flowers that my wife and father-in-law and I planted—fine things from every land. . . . "

The book John Muir wrote these words in is still in his office. After a beautiful film narrated from John Muir's text and scenes of the natural wonders that inspired it, visitors go through Muir's large 19th-century farmhouse, one of the most authentically presented houses you can visit. The closets are still filled with clothing. Muir's suitcase is on the bed, ready for travel; his glasses and pencils are on the desk in his "scribble den." Pictures of his friends President Theodore Roosevelt and naturalist John Burroughs are on the walls, and you can look through some of the scrapbooks in the parlor. You can go up to the treasure-filled attic and ring the ranch bell in the belltower.

The **Martinez Adobe**, built by the son of the Mexican don for whom the town was named, is in the garden, where you an wander at will. Muir's daughter and her family lived there, as did the ranch foreman.

Muir has written: "Climb the mountains and get their good tidings. Nature's peace will flow into you as sunshine flows into trees. The winds blow their open freshness into you, and the storms their energy, while cares will drop off like autumn leaves."

Black Diamond Mines Regional Preserve

Route 1, P.O. Box 1402, Antioch, CA 9509. Take Highway 4 to Somersville Road in Antioch, and head south on Somersville Road toward the hills. (415) 757-2620. One- and two-hour tours by reservation. (415) 757-2620. Children under 7 not permitted underground. Ages 12–61, $2; 7–11 and over 62, $1. Miner's hard hats and lights provided; wear a jacket and sturdy shoes.

Black Diamond Mines Regional Preserve was the site of 19th-century coal mining and 20th-century sand mining activity. The Hazel-Atlas sand mine on the property has been preserved as an underground mining museum for your enjoyment. It's the only place in the area where you can go into a mine and walk through the tunnels.

The surrounding 3,612-acre preserve was once a thriving town. Now, only Rose Hill cemetery, ruins, and trails remain.

Pittsburgh Historical Society
40 Civic Avenue off Richmond, Pittsburg. (415) 439-9783. Sunday 1–5, and by appointment. Donation.

The motto of this museum is: "Were it not for the preservation of memorabilia, the history of this area would fade and pass without record." Gifts from local families have helped make this collection a fine one.

The Peninsula and San Jose Area

The Peninsula and San Jose area provides many days of happy "attraction" hunting. From the huge amusement park, Great America, to small historical museums such as Lathrop House in Redwood City, the area is full of surprises. Since the area grows more crowded and less suburban, city street maps are especially helpful.

Sanchez Adobe
1000 Linda Mar Boulevard, off Highway 1, Pacifica. (415) 359-1462. Tuesday and Sunday 1–5, and by appointment. Free.

In 1842, the *alcalde,* or mayor, of San Francisco, Señor Sanchez, built his home in the farmland that once produced food for San Francisco's Mission Dolores. The adobe still stands, filled with artifacts from the Costanoan Indians who lived here first, Sanchez's rancho mementos, and the Victorian furniture and clothes of several Sanchez generations. Today's youngsters can participate in hands-on programs such as adobe brick making, Indian games, and an Indian skills workshop.

Coyote Point Museum For Environmental Education
Coyote Point Park, off Peninsula Avenue from Highway 101, and from North Shore Boulevard from San Jose and San Mateo. (415) 342-7755. Wednesday–Friday 10–5, Saturday and Sunday 1–5. Closed major holidays. Fri-

Children build a tule hut at the crafts workshop at the Sanchez Adobe.

days free. Adults $1; seniors and ages 6–17, 50¢. W. Car gate fee for park, picnic areas, playgrounds, and beach: $3.

Devoted to the understanding and appreciation of nature and our place in it—with special emphasis on the history, resources, and environmental relationships within the area—the museum offers tours of its animal center, the foothills, local tidepools, and exhibits in the center. Here visitors will learn about the beauty of the natural world through an aquarium, computer games, full-scale models, live animal displays, and films.

Japanese Tea Garden
Central Park, San Mateo. (415) 377-4700. Monday–Friday 8:30–4, Saturday and Sunday 11–5. Free.

This proper, gracious Japanese garden is a soothing spot in the midst of city bustle. Quaint bridges and rock pathways take the visitor past a waterfall, a pond thick with water lillies and goldfish, and, in springtime, pink cherry blossoms. The teahouse is open, irregularly, in summer.

*The secrets of the bottom of the sea are
revealed at the Coyote Point Museum.*

San Mateo County Historical Museum

1700 West Hillsdale Boulevard, College of San Mateo, San Mateo. Off Highway 101. (415) 574-6441. Monday–Thursday 9:30–4:30, Sunday 12:30–4:30. Free.

A walk through this museum is a walk through history. You begin with the Pleistocene period—14 million years ago—and view bones and fossils from that age found in San Mateo. Then on to the Costanoan Indians of 3,000 years ago, and the description of their magic dances, boats, tools, and food. The Mission Rancho period is well represented. Exhibits of lumber mills, an old general store and bar, settlers' wagons, and unicycles recall the past. Galleries change exhibits to focus on such subjects as 19th-century fire-fighting, the many missions of San Mateo, and transportation.

Marine Ecological Institute

1200 Chesapeake Drive, Redwood City. (415) 364-2760. $450.

*This Tree of Life shows who eats what at
the Coyote Point Museum.*

"I enjoyed geo/chem—using the VanDorn bottle to get water samples and sticking your fingers in 'Benthic Ooze'! I liked putting out the otter net and catching the fish and giving birth to some fish. I thought that looking at Phytoplankton, Zooplankton, and Circumplankton was fun." This is one San Jose student's response to the four-hour Discovery Voyage on the 85-foot research vessel *Inland Seas*. Groups of 40 to 45, over ten years old, learn about marsh and marine life and the sea around us.

Filoli House and Gardens

Filoli Nature Hikes: (415) 366-4640. Monday, Thursday, and Saturday at 9:30 by reservation. Adults $3; children, with adult only, $1.

Walk through the house and garden that star in TV's "Dynasty": 43 rooms of Georgian-style mansion and 17 acres of formal gardens.

In Filoli's gardens you can learn about the Indians who lived in the area; touch the San Andreas fault line; and learn about the animals, plants, and history of the area. The two-hour hikes are two or three miles long.

The nearby *Woodside Store* is a more rustic attraction: a store built in 1854, a museum of the actual things lumbermen and settlers would purchase in days gone by. A slide show is available on request. (Tripp and King's Mountain Road, off Highway 84, Woodside; 415-851-7615; Tuesday, Thursday, Saturday, and Sunday. 12–5; tours by appointment; free).

West Bay Model Railroad Club

1090 Merrill Street, Menlo Park. (415) 322-0685. Free.

Three different-sized trains run on the club's 2,000 feet of track, whistling past miniature towns and painted scenery and over tiny bridges and turntables. Adding to the effectiveness of the show is a tape of special sound effects interspersed with the story of how the club came about. The club also has a railroad-stationery display, a library, and a workshop. The members' special Christmas show on the second weekend in December is a favorite with local youngsters.

Stanford University

Stanford University Campus, Stanford. Highway 101 to Stanford exit. (415) 723-2300. Stanford Guide and Visitors Service (723-2560/723-2053): Monday–Sunday 10–4 when school is in session. Hoover Tower Observation

Platform (723-2053): Monday–Sunday 10–11:45 and 1–4. Adults $1, children and seniors 50¢, families $2.50. Leland Stanford, Jr. Museum (723-3469): Tuesday–Friday 10–5, Saturday and Sunday 1–5. Free. **Stanford Linear Accelerator Center** *(926-3300, ext. 2204): tours by appointment; free.* **Jasper Ridge Biological Preserve** *(327-2277): tours by appointment; free.*

In addition to the lovely aerial view from the tower, the **Hoover Institution** offers memories of Herbert Hoover and his White House years and world crusades. A settee and chairs that belonged to Abraham Lincoln are also on display. Remembrances of the Stanford family are displayed in the **Leland Stanford, Jr. Museum,** along with a widely varied collection including Rodin sculptures, Indian artifacts, European and primitive art and sculpture, and an Egyptorium with a mummy in an open case. The Stanford Room features toy trains and soldiers; a check signed by George Washington; Leland, Jr.'s archaelogical findings from Pompeii; Mrs. Stanford's gowns; and the gold spike driven in by Leland Stanford to complete the first transcontinental railroad in 1869.

Baylands Nature Interpretive Center

2775 Embarcadero Road, at the eastern end, Palo Alto. (415) 329-2506. Wednesday–Friday 2–5, weekends 1–5. Free. (Mail c/o Palo Alto Junior Museum.)

This bayside nature center is on pilings out in a salt marsh, handy for the nature walks and ecology workshops it excels in. The exhibits show local birds, plants, and a saltwater aquarium. On weekends, there are nature movies and slide shows, as well as nature and bird walks, bike tours, wildflower shows, fish, pond, and geology programs and workshops.

Palo Alto Junior Museum and Zoo

Rinconada Park, 1451 Middlefield Road, downtown Palo Alto. (415) 329-2111. Tuesday–Friday 10–12 and 1–5, Saturday 10–5, Sunday 1–4. W. Free.

This beautifully constructed museum has constantly changing exhibits to keep kids coming back for more. Outside, in the poured-concrete shelters, there are snakes and reptiles, ravens, owls and foxes, and lovable rabbits.

Ducks nest under the bridge that curves over the pretty ponds. The exhibitions program focuses on physical, biological, and earth science.

Barbie Doll Hall of Fame
Doll Studio, 325 Hamilton, Palo Alto. From downtown turn left at Middlefield Road to Hamilton, then right on Hamilton. (415) 326-5841. Tuesday–Saturday 10:15–5. Adults $1, children 50¢.

The world's largest collection of Barbie Dolls—14,000 Barbies and Kens—includes the first Black Barbie, a hippie Barbie, Barbie as the first woman astronaut, Barbie as a yuppie, and other incarnations reflecting the changing fashion in clothes, accessories, and hairstyles over the last quarter century.

Foothill Electronics Museum
Foothill College, El Monte Road at I-280, Los Altos Hills. North West corner of campus, adjacent to the Observatory. (415) 960-4393. Thursday and Friday 9:30–4:40, Sunday 1–4, and by appointment. W. Free.

Based on a private collection started in 1893 by six-year-old Douglas Perham, this is the most extensive display of early electrical and electronic devices in the west. Young scientists will be intrigued by exhibits of the first radio broadcasting station, the first Silicon Valley electronics firm, the first TV picture tube (invented by Philo Farnsworth in San Francisco), a ten-foot robot, and hands-on demonstrations of electricity and magnetism.

Engine House
672 Alberta, near Hollenbach and Fremont, Sunnyvale. (408) 245-0609. Wednesday–Friday 12–5, Saturday 10–5, Sunday 12–5, later in summer and before Christmas.

One million items ("the next million we have on order") of interest to train fans are crammed into this treasure-filled space. Cars, kits, photos, hobby magazines, models of trains from old wood-burners to BART, and everything you'd need to create a complete train world can be found in the largest train shop in the west.

Nearby, the **Sunnyvale Historical Museum** captures the past with artifacts and pictures of the pioneers (235 East California, Sunnyvale; 408-

Twentieth century kids play with seventeenth century toys used by the first Californians at the California History Center, De Anza College.

749-0220; Tuesday and Thursday 12–3:30, Sunday 1–4, and by appointment; free).

California History Center
De Anza College, 21250 Stevens Creek Boulevard, Cupertino. (408) 996-4712. Monday–Friday 8–12 and 1–4:30, Saturday 10–2. Closed July and August. Free.

Changing exhibits—from "First Californians" to "The Chinese in the Monterey Bay Area" to "Hard Rock Gold Mining"—explore California's rich and varied history. Children also enjoy a hands-on experience during their visit. This living history museum is housed in the restored Le Petit Trianon, the original house on De Anza land. Visitors may also tour this elegant Louis XVI mansion with a pavilion reminiscent of Versailles.

Minolta Planetarium
De Anza College, 21250 Stevens Creek Boulevard and Stelling Road, Cupertino. (408) 996-4814. Call for times and prices, since they change with each class session.

The Minolta Planetarium uses the latest audiovisual equipment and techniques to present remarkable shows. The main projector spreads the night sky across a 50-foot dome, and 24 sound speakers and 150 other projectors produce dazzling effects: you can fly to the moon to look at the brilliance of the stars as they were seen by the astronauts, then travel back in time to see how the stars looked when humans first saw them.

Hakone Japanese Gardens
21000 Big Basin Way, Saratoga. (408) 867-3438, ext. 50. Monday–Friday 10–5, weekends 11–5. Closed holidays. 25¢. Children under 10 must be accompanied by an adult.

Walk along curving foliage-lined paths and through a wisteria-roofed arbor; step on three stones to get across a stream next to three waterfalls. Climb a moon bridge to see the goldfish. Discover a moon-viewing house and gazebos hidden in the trees. Spy stone and wooden lanterns and statues of cranes and cats hidden in the flowers. This wonderful garden was designed by a former court gardener to the Emperor of Japan as a hill and water garden in the strolling-pond style typical of Zen gardens in the 17th century. The Teahouse is open by appointment.

Villa Montalvo

Saratoga-Los Gatos Road, Saratoga. (408) 741-3421. Arboretum, Monday– Friday 8–5, weekends 9–5. Galleries: Thursday–Friday 1–4, weekends 11- 4. Free.

Nature trails traverse a redwood grove, hills and meadows, and flower-covered arbors in this arboretum. The villa's grounds are also a bird sanctuary for 41 species of birds. The villa takes its name from a 16th-century Spanish author. Montalvo wrote a novel describing a tribe of Amazons living in a fabulous island paradise named California. The Amazons rode on gryphons, and the many stone gryphons on the grounds will entrance youngsters. Music, dance, and other performing arts events are scheduled in spring and summer and at Christmas.

Billy Jones Wildcat Railroad

Oak Meadow Park, Los Gatos. For tours and special runs, write to 649 University Avenue, Los Gatos 95030. (408) 395-9775. Open Easter vacation, spring and fall weekends, Tuesday–Saturday 11–5:30 and Sunday 12–5:30 in summer. 75¢.

"Old Number 2," a full-steam, narrow-gauge, 18-inch prairie-type locomotive, toots along a mile-long track pulling four open cars. The water tank, a necessity when operating a steam railroad, was designed and built by volunteers, as were the turntable, station, and engine house.

Campbell Historical Museum

51 North Central, off First Street and Civic Center Drive, Campbell. (408) 866-2119. Tuesday–Saturday 1:30–4:30. Closed holidays. Free.

Changing exhibits such as "A Woman's Work Is Never Done," which explores the changes in homemaking in a well-equipped Santa Clara Valley home from the 1800s to 1900s, reveal the past and help us to understand the present.

Mission Santa Clara De Asis

University of Santa Clara, the Alameda, 820 Alviso, Santa Clara. (408) 984-4242. Daily 8-5. Free.

Founded in 1777 and now part of the university campus, the present mission is a replica of the third building raised on this site by the mission fathers. An adobe wall from the original cloister still stands in the peaceful garden. The original cross of the mission stands in front of the church, and the bell given by the King of Spain in 1778 still tolls.

The **de Saisset Art Museum** (Tuesday–Friday 10–5, weekends 1–5; 544-4545) and **Ricard Observatory** (Wednesday 10–2) are on campus and make interesting short stops.

Great America

Great America Parkway, off Highway 101, Santa Clara. (408) 988-1800. 10–9 spring and fall weekends and daily in summer, later on Saturday and holiday weekends. Adults $15.95; children 3–6, $7.95; over 55, $9.95. Season passes: $42.50. Tickets available at BASS outlets. W.

The thrill-ride capital of Northern California offers new experiments in the fast and scary, such as Revolution, a passenger ship that swings like a pendulum until everyone is upside down; The Edge, where you fall from a tall tower at 55 miles an hour; Demon, an especially-jolting roller coaster; and Grizzly, an old-fashioned wooden roller coaster. At Fort Fun, kids can meet costumed cartoon characters such as Yogi Bear and Fred Flintstone and watch a puppet theater or ride Little Dodge 'Ems, Lady Bugs, and Huck's Hang Gliders. Concerts, the Salt Water Circus, and stage shows allow for pleasant respites during a day, or night, of adventure.

Rosicrucian Egyptian Museum, Science Museum, and Planetarium

Rosicrucian Park, Naglee and Park avenues, San Jose. (408) 287-9171. Egyptian Museum: Tuesday–Sunday 9–5. Adults, $3; senior citizens $2.50; children 12–17, $1; children under 12 free. Science Museum and Planetarium; Monday–Friday 1–4:30, weekends 12–4:30, in summer: Monday–Friday 10–4:30, weekends 12–4:30. Shows at 2 p.m. Monday–Friday, weekends 2 and 3:30, in summer: 2 and 3:30 daily. Adults $2; seniors $1.50; children 7–18, $1. Closed August 2, Thanksgiving, Christmas, and New Year's Day. Group discounts and special shows by appointment.

The facade of the Rosicrucian Egyptian Museum is a reproduction of the Avenue of Ram Sphinxes from the Karnac Temple in Thebes, Egypt. Taurt, the statue in the center, is the predynastic hippopotamus deity known as the protectress of women. Her name means the Great One.

The wonderful, faraway world of ancient Egypt awaits to mystify and enchant you in an amazingly large and varied collection. Egyptian and Babylonian mummies, sculpture, paintings, jewelry, cosmetics, scarabs, scrolls, and amulets are here in abundance. The ornate coffins, mummified cats and falcons, and descriptions of the embalming process are totally absorbing—especially to youngsters, who want to know how old everything is. Sumerian clay tablets; a model of the Tower of Babel; a diorama of the Paleolithic Period, 25,000 years ago, including original tools; and a walk-through Egyptian noble's tomb vie for your attention.

Next door in the **Science Museum**, lifelike models of satellites and neighboring planets come to life with push buttons in the many active exhibits, which include a working seismograph and a Foucault pendulum.

The Rosicrucian Planetarium, a theater of the sky, presents changing

The Rosicrucian Planetarium offers exciting Theatre of the Sky programs for a clearer understanding of the wonders of the heavens.

programs exploring the myths, mysteries, and facts of the sky of yesterday, today, and tomorrow.

Winchester Mystery House

525 South Winchester Boulevard, between Stevens Creek and I-280, San Jose. (408) 247-2101. One-hour tours daily except Christmas 9:30–4:30 in winter, 9–5:30 in summer. Adults $9.95; 60 and over $8.95; children 6–12, $5.95. Reduced group tour and catering rates (in Sarah's Cafe) by reservation.

Sarah Winchester, widow of the Winchester Rifle heir, was told that as long as she kept building something, she'd never die. So for 38 years, carpenters worked 24 hours a day to build this 160-room mansion filled with mysteries. Doorways open to blank walls, secret passageways twist around, and the number 13 appears everywhere—13-stepped stairways, ceilings with

13 panels, room with 13 windows—all in the finest woods and crystals money could buy.

A self-guided tour of the Victorian Gardens, Winchester Historical Firearms Museum, and the Antique Products Museum is included in the tour price.

San Jose Historical Museum

635 Phelan Avenue, San Jose, in the southernmost section of Kelley Park at Senator Road. (408) 287-2290. Monday–Friday 10–4:30, weekends 12–4:30. Adults $2, children $1, seniors $1.50. Group rates, by appointment.

Reconstructed and restored landmarks bring to life the look and feel of late-19th-century San Jose in this 16-acre complex. Walk around the plaza and visit O'Brien's Candy Store (in 1878 the first place to serve ice cream sodas west of Detroit), the print shop, the 1880s Pacific Hotel, Dashaway Stables, the 115-foot Electric Light Tower, the Empire Firehouse, a 1927 Gas Station, Coyote Post Office, Steven's Ranch Fruit Barn, H.H. Warburton's Doctor's Office, the 1909 Bank of Italy building, and the many Victorian homes that have been saved and moved to museum premises.

Japanese Friendship Tea Garden

1300 Senter Road, Kelley Park, San Jose. (408) 277-5254. Daily 10–sunset. Free.

This tranquil garden is patterned after the Korakuen garden in San Jose's sister city of Okayama. The three lakes are designed to symbolize the word *kokoro,* which means "heart-mind-and-soul." Picturesque bridges and waterfalls, shaped rocks and trees, and land and water flowers are wonderful to wander among. Naturally, the children will head over to watch the families of *koi,* fat gold, white, or black carp who come when dinner is offered.

Happy Hollow Park and Zoo

1300 Senter Road, on the northern side of Kelley Park, San Jose. (408) 295-8188/292-8383. Usually open 10–5, but call to be sure. Adults $2; ages 2–14 and over 65, $1.50. Groups by reservation. W.

See a dragon prowl a trail through a bamboo forest, or listen as a chorus of sea animals invites you to enter King Neptune's kingdom. Climb a stairway

Once one enters the Magic Castle at
Happy Hollow Park and Zoo, magical
things can happen.

in the Crooked House and slide down a spiral slide. Visit the many mazes and play areas dotting the park and view a puppet show at the puppet castle theater. The zoo offers youngsters a chance to see exotic animals from all over the world. They can cuddle a baby goat or pet a baby llama.

Youth Scientific Institute

16260 Alum Rock Avenue, off Highway 680 to Alum Park, San Jose. (408) 258-4322. Tuesday–Friday 9–4:30, Saturday 12–4:30, summer Sunday (in summer only) 11–5:30. Adults 50¢, children 10¢, families $1. W. Picnic tables, play areas, and children's programs.

A small petting area, a large display of stuffed birds, and a hands-on exhibit of whale bones and shark teeth will draw the children, as will the living hawks, owls, kestrels, snakes, newts, skunks, boa constrictors, and chinchillas in the animal rehabilitation center.

New Almaden Quicksilver Mining Museum

21570 Almaden Road, P.O. Box 124, New Almaden. (408) 268-1729. Saturday 12–4. $1.

Until the County Park Association opens its new museum on the site of the old mine office in the Hacienda furnace yard, the Original New Almaden Mercury Mining Museum of mining artifacts gathered by Constance Perham, who as a young girl accompanied her father on trips to the mines, serves as a fascinating reminder of the early settlers.

Flying Lady II Restaurant and Wagons to Wings Museum
15060 Foothill Road, Morgan Hill. (408) 779-4136/227-4607. Lunch and dinner Wednesday–Sunday. Sunday Dixieland Jazz Brunch. Moderate prices. Museum open Wednesday–Sunday, 10 a.m.–8 p.m. Free.

One of the world's largest restaurants, the Flying Lady II is an adventure in dining. Seven full-sized antique aircraft hang over the spectacular main dining room, along with over 100 scale-model airplanes "flying" over diners on a moving track. Antique flags of the world and merry-go-round horses add to the colorful atmosphere.

The Wagons to Wings Museum is home to antique cars, aircraft and horse-drawn wagons, including the 1929 Ford Tri-Motor seen in the movie *Indiana Jones and the Temple of Doom*.

Gilroy Historical Museum
195 Fifth Street, at Church, Gilroy. (408) 847-2685. Tuesday–Friday 9–12 and 1–5, Saturday 1–5. Closed holidays. Donation.

Telephones, tools, and toys are just part of this collection of over 10,000 donated memories from Gilroy's pioneer families.

Lick Observatory
Mount Hamilton, Highway 130, 25 miles southeast of San Jose. (408) 274-5060/429-2513. Gallery 10–5 daily; tours 2–5. Closed holidays. Free.

A long, narrow winding road takes you to the top of Mount Hamilton and the awesome domes of Lick Observatory. It was here that four of the 16 known satellites of Jupiter were discovered—the first ones found since the time of Galileo. Now star clusters and galaxies are studied with the most modern equipment. The visitors' gallery looks up at one of the largest telescopes (120 inches) in the world, and the tour of photos and astronomical instruments is intriguing and educational. Star gazing is possible for the public on summer Fridays, but you must write, enclosing a self-addressed, stamped envelope for 1 to 6 tickets, to Visitors Program, Lick Observatory, Mt. Hamilton, CA 95140.

Public Relations Tours

☐ **Acres of Orchids.** *Rod McLellan Orchidary, 1450 El Camino Real, South San Francisco. (415) 871-5655. Guided tours 10:30 and 1:30 daily.* Orchids in more colors, types, and sizes than you can imagine are here for looking, smelling, and buying.

☐ **U.S. Weather Service** *Bayshore Freeway, San Bruno, S. F. International Airport. (415) 876-2886.* See the materials used in briefing pilots and the weather teletypes and instruments. Free tours, by appointment. To see *San Francisco Airport* itself, call 761-0800 to arrange for a free 90-minute tour.

☐ **Palo Alto Airport.** *1925 Embarcadero Road, Palo Alto. (415) 856-8080/127. By appointment. Free.*

☐ **Sunset Magazine.** *Middlefield and Willow roads, Menlo Park, 1 mile southwest of Highway 101. (415) 321-3600. Free building tours Monday–Friday at 10:30, 11:30, 1, 2, and 3. Groups by appointment. Gardens open 8–4:30.* Lane Publishing Company is the headquarters for *Sunset* Magazine, books, films, and television. Budding journalists can see editorial offices, test kitchens, patios, and office entertainment areas. They can also enjoy the *Sunset* gardens: when you walk on a path from one end to the other, you view, in order, the botanical life of the western coast of America—from Northwest rhododendrons and azaleas to the cactus of the desert.

☐ **Nasa Ames Research Center.** *Highway 101. (415) 965-6497. Free 1½-two-hour tours, by appointment, Monday–Friday 9–3:30, for those over 9 years old.* After an orientation lecture and film, visitors can see the world's largest wind tunnel, centrifuge operations, research aircraft, or flight-simulation facilities, depending on the center's schedule. Films, tele-lectures, and school presentations are also available by calling 694-6270/5543.

Hands-on fun at the Santa Cruz City Museum.

Heading South by the Sea

The Santa Cruz Area

The Santa Cruz area is small, nestled on a bay southwest of San Jose and north of Monterey. Big Basin Redwoods, Boulder Creek, and Natural Bridges and Loch Lomond state parks are some of the natural sites of interest, and the towns of Watsonville and Castroville, home of the artichoke, are perfect day trips. Here are spots for bird watching, butterfly watching, whale watching, herb and heritage walks, or sky and sea walks. In Santa Cruz, beaches are the main attraction. Be sure to bring along car games to wile away the two-hour ride from San Francisco. Highway 1, along the coast, is more beautiful and more curving than the faster Highway 101.

William H. Volck Memorial Museum
261 East Beach Street, Watsonville. (408) 772-0305. Tuesday–Thursday 11–3, and by appointment. Free.

Local history is lovingly preserved in this community museum featuring items and artifacts from the Pajaro Valley. We like the fine collection of historic costumes and textiles, from gingham sunbonnets and aprons to opera hats and ballgowns.

This 335,000-gallon exhibit presents a diver's view of a towering kelp forest community. As giant kelp need sunlight and wave motion to survive, the 29-foot-high tank is open to the sky at the Monterey Bay Aquarium.

Lighthouse Surfing Museum
West Cliff Drive, Santa Cruz. (408) 429-3773/429-3429. Daily 11–4, 12–5 in summer. Free.

The Santa Cruz Surfing Museum, the only surfing museum on the planet, is located in the Mark Abbott Memorial Lighthouse on Lighthouse Point overlooking Steamer's Lane, the best surfboard inlet in the area. On display are photographs, surfboards, and other surfing memorabilia tracing more than 50 years of surfing in the Santa Cruz area.

Long Marine Laboratory and Aquarium
Off Delaware Avenue, near Natural Bridges State Park, Santa Cruz. (408) 426-4087. Group tours by appointment. Free.

A marine research facility of the University of California at Santa Cruz, this is a working laboratory featuring fascinating tidepool aquariums, touch tanks, the skeleton of an 85-foot blue whale, a dolphinarium, and a glimpse of current research. Tidepool exploration tours are also available.

The Mystery Spot
1953 Banciforte Drive, Santa Cruz. (408) 423-8897. Daily 9:30–4:30. Adults $3; children under 11, $1.50. Tours and group rates.

All the laws of gravity are challenged in this scary natural curiosity. Balls roll up hill, trees can't stand up straight, and you always seem to be standing either backwards or sideways. One test here is to lay a carpenter's level across two cement blocks, checking to see that their tops are on the same level. Then stand on one and see your friend on the other suddenly shrink or grow tall. You can also walk up the walls of a cabin that looks cockeyed, but isn't. Alice in Wonderland's caterpillar would feel right at home.

Santa Cruz Beach and Boardwalk
400 Beach Street at Riverside Avenue, Santa Cruz. (408) 423-5590. Daily 11–10 in summer, until 11 on Saturday; weekends and holidays 11–5 (except Christmas) in spring and fall. Ticket books $3–$6. All-day ride tickets $10.95. Group rates; picnic areas by reservation for groups. General admission is free.

The Giant Dipper, one of the world's top ten roller coasters, and the classic 1911 Looff Merry-Go-Round, with 62 hand-carved wooden horses, vie for popularity at California's only remaining beach amusement park. The last of the old-time boardwalks, Santa Cruz has everything you'd hope to find on one: a Ferris wheel, bumper cars, skeet ball, a penny-video arcade, miniature golf, cotton candy, sweet and scary rides—including the new Video storm and the Wave Jammer. There are 19 restaurants and fast food

The Giant Dipper at the Santa Cruz Beach Boardwalk is rated one of the top ten roller coasters in the world.

vendors, and the best thing of all, a wonderful white beach. Popeye and his family greet summer visitors daily.

On the pier nearby, you can fish and see sea lions swimming around the pilings.

Santa Cruz City Museum

1305 East Cliff Drive at Pilkington, Santa Cruz. (408) 429-3773. Tuesday– Saturday, 10–5, Sunday 12–5. Tourists $1, residents 50¢; children and seniors free. Reserved parking on Pilkington in summer.

A "gray whale" welcomes you to natural history exhibits of animals, birds, and local plant groups. Learn how local Ohlone Indians lived, and grind acorns in a stone mortar. See a mastodon skull from a prehistoric denizen of the region. Touch live tidepool animals. You can picnic in the park that surrounds the museum, or build a sand castle on the beach across the street. A slide show on the geology of Santa Cruz is given on request. Seasonal group tours by appointment.

You might also enjoy a stop at the **Santa Cruz Arts Center** on Center

Starfish are just some of the wonderful creatures in the tidepool at the Santa Cruz City Museum.

Street downtown, or the small **Historical Museum of Santa Cruz** in the octagon-shaped Old County Hall, 118 Cooper at Front Street (408-425-2540; Monday–Saturday 10–5, free).

The kids will be right at home in the **Children's Art Foundation**, which collects, preserves, and exhibits children's art from around the world; published **Stone Soup**, a magazine of writing and art by children; and gives art lessons (915 Cedar Street; 408-426-5557, Monday–Friday 2–5:30, and by appointment, free).

Roaring Camp & Big Trees Narrow-Gauge Railroad and Santa Cruz, Big Trees & Pacific Railway Company

Highway 17 to Mt. Hermon Road exit in Scotts Valley, then west 3½ miles to the end of the road at Felton, left onto Graham Hill Road (P.O. Box G-1, Felton CA 95018). (408) 335-4400. Roaring Camp round-trip fares: Ages 3–15, $7.50 over 16, $10.50. Santa Cruz, Big Trees round trip: $8.50 and $16. Group rates available. Call for schedules.

Old train buffs now have two fabulous train rides to choose from, both originating at Roaring Camp. Great steam locomotives hiss and puff through the redwoods on the steepest narrow-gauge railroad grade in North America around the tightest of turns to the top of Big Mountain. The 1¼-hour trip transports riders back 100 years. On the two-hour Picnic Line between Roaring Camp and the Santa Cruz beaches, passengers ride in historic 1902 wooden and 1926 steel passenger cars and open-vista and one way. Back in Roaring Camp, you can explore an 1880s logging town, wander along nature trails, rest beside an 1840s covered bridge, chow down at the Chuck Wagon Bar-B-Cue, and, on summer weekends, laugh at the Roaring Camp Melodrama Players.

Public Relations Tours

□ **Salz Tannery Tour** *1040 River Street, Santa Cruz. (408) 423-1480. Tours by appointment. Free.* The oldest tannery west of Chicago, Salz produces fine leather goods and accessories.

*The engineer readies the track for the
Roaring Camp Railroad trip through the
redwoods.*

The Monterey Area

Since its discovery in 1542 by Spanish explorer Juan Cabrillo, the Monterey Peninsula has been a mecca for vagabonds and visionaries, pioneers in agriculture and art. It was here that California, after being under the flags of Spain and Mexico, became part of the United States. The Monterey area offers many things worth investigating: an Arcadian seashore in Big Sur, a small city filled with history evoking memories of John Steinbeck, a sweeping windswept valley now turning into fertile farmland. Here you can go hang gliding, ballooning, tidepooling, or on nature walks. Allow three hours driving time going south on Highway 101 to the Monterey turn-off, or 3½ hours by the prettier coast route.

San Juan Bautista State Historic Park
Highway 156 off Highway 101, San Juan Bautista. (408) 623-4881. Daily 10–4:30 in winter, until 5 in summer. Adults $1, children 50¢. Separate do-

nation for the mission. Tours by appointment. Check at ranger station for scheduled interpretive activities. Call for information on Living History Days, when volunteers don period costumes and re-enact events from California's past.

A mission, a museum, an adobe house, an 1870s hotel and stables, a washhouse, a blacksmith shop, a granary, and a cabin are grouped around the lovely plaza of San Juan Bautista, representing three periods in California history: Spanish, Mexican, and Early Californian.

Start your visit at the **Mission,** founded in 1797 and carefully preserved. The old adobe rooms house many treasures, including a 1737 barrel organ, gaming sticks of the San Juan Indians, and artifacts from the original building. The original bells still call parishioners to Mass. In the mission gardens, today's youngsters can learn the same things the Indians were taught: weaving, candlemaking, and baking.

Cross to the **Castro Adobe,** which also houses General Castro's secretary's office. This should serve as a model for other museums: every room

Buckboards are great for climbing at San Juan Bautista.

is completely labeled, with pictures to aid in the identification of the objects. The house is furnished as it was in the 1870s by the Breen family, who survived the Donner Party disaster to find a fortune in the goldfields. You'll see the candlesticks that came west with the Breens, and the diary, wardrobe, wedding dress, gloves, fan, and card case of Isabella Breen. The kitchen is complete right down to the boot pull.

The Plaza Hotel, next door, is noted for its barroom, with billiard and poker tables standing ready. Built in 1813 as a barracks for the Spanish soldiers, the walls now display Wells Fargo memorabilia and photos of the pioneers, and the slide show brings "the early years" to life.

You can visit a completely furnished Victorian home, with dishes on the table and a singing bird in the parlor. Diagonally across the Plaza is the **Zanetta House**, built on the foundation of the adobe that once housed the Indian maidens of the settlement. The **Livery Stables** are jammed with wonderful wagons including a surrey with a fringe on top, an Amish buggy by Studebaker, a "tally ho wagon," phaetons, and buckboards.

The streets nearby have interesting shops and restaurants, making San Juan Bautista a perfect place to spend a relaxing morning or afternoon.

San Luis Reservoir
Romero Overlook, Highway 152, 15 miles west of Los Banos. (209) 826-0718, ext. 53. Daily 9–5. Closed major holidays. Free.

In the Romero Overlook, pictures, graphic wall displays, movies, and slide shows tell the story of the State Water Project and the Federal Central Valley Project, and how they work together at the San Luis Complex. Telescopes at the center offer a spectacular view of the area. The visitor center is staffed by Water Resources guides.

Monterey

In this bustling port town, the path of history meanders gently next to natural attractions and busy shops. Fisherman's Wharf is a mélange of restaurants, fish stores and shops, but seal watching is the favored pastime, and you can go for a boat ride or take a diving bell 30 feet down to look at the ocean floor. There are also picnic tables near the bocce ball courts.

Today's Cannery Row is a far cry from the Cannery Row in John Steinbeck's books. Now it's a growing complex of restaurants, shops, and galleries offering entertainment for all. Overlooking the Row is the

Edgewater Packing Company, with its Gay 90s Carousel, family arcade, factory-outlet complex and ice cream and pie restaurant. (Prescott and Foam avenues; (408) 649-1899; daily 11–11, later in summer).

Spirit of Monterey Wax Museum
700 Cannery Row, Monterey. (408) 375-3770. Daily, 11–8, longer hours in summer. Adults $5, children 6–16 and adults over 65, $3. Student tours and rates, by appointment. W.

Dozens of scenes tell the spellbinding story of the Monterey area and the people who lived it, from the Indians who lived here before the Spanish galleons cast anchor, to Steinbeck's rowdy crew and Clint Eastwood, ex-mayor of Carmel. Here visitors meet Concepción, who fell in love with a Russian officer and waited in vain for his return; Robert Louis Stevenson; the Spanish dons who ruled Monterey; and Thomas Larkin, California's first "ambassador" to the United States. Kit Carson rides up and tells his story, Joaquin Murietta recites poetry, and Steinbeck reminisces about his friends in the Lone Star Cafe.

Monterey Bay Aquarium
886 Cannery Row, Monterey. (408) 649-6466. Daily 10–6, except Christmas. Adults $7; students and seniors $5; children 3–12, $3. Posted feeding schedules. Regularly scheduled workshops and discovery labs. Group rates and tours available.

"He's feeding fish to fish!" one youngster exclaimed, while standing entranced before the three-story kelp forest. All the wonders of a hidden world come to light at the internationally acclaimed Monterey Bay Aquarium, one of California's "top ten" attractions. In a startling undersea tour of Monterey Bay, visitors will meet 600 living species in 23 habitat galleries and exhibits. California sea otters frolic nose to nose with you in their own pool, visible on three different levels. You can investigate with telescopes and microscopes, play with bat rays and starfish, or walk through a shorebird aviary. Did you know that a baby blue whale drinks 130 gallons of milk a day? Or that a blue whale eats 3 million calories of shrimplike krill a day—the equivalent of 8,000 Big Macs? Films, slide shows, and hands-on interpretive exhibits challenge and intrigue. The aquarium is outstanding, a beautifully designed treat for the whole family.

A hands-on exhibit, the touch tide pool, provides an array of sea stars, chitons, mussels, decorator crabs, and various other tidepool creatures for visitors to touch and investigate at the Monterey Bay Aquarium.

Dennis the Menace Playground
El Estero City park, off Del Monte Avenue, Camino del Estero and Fremont. Open during daylight hours. Free.

Youngsters will want to head to the colorful *Dennis the Menace Playground,* designed by cartoonist Hank Ketchum. Here little potential "menaces" can let off steam in a steam switch engine, hang from the Umbrella Tree, sweep down the Giant Swing Ride, and put their heads in the lion's mouth for a drink of water.

Allen Knight Maritime Museum
550 Calle Principal, Monterey. (408) 375-2553. Tuesday–Friday 1–4, 10– 4 in summer; weekends, 2–4. Groups by appointment. Free.

*This sweet sea lion is a happy inhabitant
at the Monterey Bay Aquarium.*

A captain's cabin from an old sailing ship, with a bed, a writing desk, and a sailor's ditty box, sets the proper mood for this nautical museum. Models, photos, lithographs, paintings, and various old sailing accoutrements: octants, ships' bells, sailors' thimbles, Arctic goggles, scrimshaw, and ships' logs are some of the items on display. One exhibit shows the historic ships that have visited Monterey harbor. There's even a sardine boat in which you can go for a pretend sail.

The City of Monterey has made it easy for visitors to see its beginnings: a yellow line, with arrows, has been painted on several of the main streets downtown. By following the yellow line, you follow **The Path of History**. Landmark plaques tell briefly who built each house, and why it's a landmark. Six of the houses along The Path of History are also part of the Monterey State Historic Park complex, and day tickets, $3.50 for adults, $2 for children, will admit you to all six adobes in the park (Larkin House, Stevenson House, Casa Soberanes, Cooper Molera, Custom House, and Pacific House). Or you an pay $1 per building for adults, 50¢ per building for children. Groups by appointment.

Sancho Panza Restaurant

Casa Gutierrez, 590 Calle Principal, Monterey. (408) 375-0095. Daily 11–2 and 5–9, later in summer.

Built in 1841 by a young Mexican for his bride, the old adobe is now a comfortable Mexican inn that feels like an early Monterey home. The father earned his living as a farmer and rancher, and raised 15 children here. Today, Casa Gutierrez is part of the Monterey State Historic park, 42 historic adobe buildings found along the Path of History. A warm fire blazes on cool evenings, and there's a garden in back for lunch and summer nights. Prices are reasonable and the food is delicious. Tortilla- and tamale-making demonstrations are scheduled with park rangers.

The Larkin House

510 Calle Principal at Jefferson Street, Monterey. (408) 649-7118. Guided tours on the hour, 10–4 daily except Tuesday. Monterey State Historic Park groups by appointment.

Built by Thomas Oliver Larkin, the first and only U.S. Consul to Mexico stationed in Monterey, Larkin House is an architectural and historical gem. It was the first home in Monterey in the two-story New England style, as well as the first to have glass windows. Many of the furnishings are original. Through the rose-covered garden is a small house, now a museum, once used by William Tecumseh Sherman, an Army lieutenant in 1847–49, who went on to become the famous Civil War general. It's said that he left a beautiful woman waiting in vain for his return.

The Stevenson House

530 Houston Street, Monterey. (408) 649-7118. Tours on the hour 10–4 daily except Wednesday.

In 1879 Robert Louis Stevenson spent a few months in a second-floor room of this boardinghouse. He had traveled from Scotland to visit Fanny Osbourne, who later became his wife. He wrote *The Old Pacific Capital* here. The house is restored to look as it did then, with several rooms devoted to Stevensonia. Be sure to see the doll collection upstairs.

Cooper-Molera Adobe
Polk and Munras streets, Monterey. (408) 649-7118. Tours on the hour, 10–4 daily except Wednesday.

This newly restored complex contains Capt. John Cooper's townhouse (he was happily married to Mariano Vallejo's sister Encarnación), several adobe buildings, period gardens, and a museum store.

Casa Sobranes
336 Pacific Street at Del Monte, Monterey. (408) 649-7118. Tours on the hour 10–4 daily except Thursday.

"The House with the Blue Gate" is an authentic, typical home of Mexican California. The furnishings reflect the blend of early New England and China trade pieces with Mexican folk art. A collection of local art graces the house as well.

The Boston Store
Corner of Scott and Oliver streets, Monterey. (408) 649-3364. Wednesday–Sunday 10–4.

Built by Thomas O. Larkin about 1845, this structure housed a general store operated by Joseph Boston & Co. in the 1850s. The building was later called Casa del Oro because it was supposed to have served as a gold depository. Today, it is again a general merchandise store operated by the Monterey History and Art Association.

The Custom House
No. 1 Custom House Plaza, Monterey. (408) 649-7118. Daily 10–4, until 5 in summer.

The United States flag was first officially raised in California on the roof of this house in 1846. It is here that each ship captain presented his cargo for the customs inspector. Today, you walk into a long room that holds the cargo Richard Henry Dana wrote about in his novel *Two Years Before the Mast*. There are casks of liquor, cases of dishes, bags of nails, coffee, flour, and wagon wheels. A screeching yellow and green parrot rules a roost of ribbons, ropes, cloth, shawls, soap, paper, tools, and trunks. In one corner, piles of "California bank notes"—cowhides—wait to be used for trading. The Custom House manager's quarters upstairs feature a comfortable carved bed and chest, a table, and a desk with an open ledger and a cigar ready to be lit.

Pacific House
No. 10 Custom House Plaza, Monterey. (408) 649-7117. Daily 10–4, until 5 in winter.

The first floor of this tavern-court-newspaper-church-ballroom is now a museum of California history, with artifact-filled cases arranged chronologically, beginning with the Costanoan Indians. Spanish saddles and money, gold miners' tools, a whaling boat, and the Victorian furniture of the pioneers are represented. Upstairs is the Holman Collection, a remarkable gathering of Indian relics from all over North America. Costanoan religion, hunting, fishing, the gathering and processing of acorns, housing, trade, transportation, warfare, and survival lessons are explained with artifacts and models. Compare the arrows, games, beads, and baskets of many tribes, from Alaskan Eskimos to American Indians.

Monterey's First Theatre/Jack Swan's Tavern
Corner of Scott and Pacific streets, Monterey. Building information (408) 375-5100. Theater information (408) 375-4916.

Jack Swan's lodging house gave its first performance of a stage play in 1847 to entertain bored soldiers. Since then, theatrical productions have been produced regularly, and now 19th-century melodramas are performed on weekends. During the day you can walk through and look at the theatrical memorabilia, including a playbill for Lola Montez. The theater company celebrated its 50th anniversary in 1987.

Colton Hall Museum of the City of Monterey
Pacific Street between Jefferson and Madison, Monterey. (408)375-9944. Daily 10–5. Free.

Colton Hall, the first town hall and public school of Monterey, was the site of the first Constitutional Congress of the State of California, in 1849. Here the California Constitution was written in Spanish and English, and the Great Seal of the state was designed. The large meeting room is furnished as it was then, with biographies and portraits of each of the men who signed the constitution, including Larkin, Vallejo, Ellis, Sutter, and Ord. A 26-star flag still flies.

Behind Colton Hall is the **Old Monterey Jail**, open daily until 4:30. The two-foot-thick walls are granite, the doors iron, and the cells scary. Believe it or not, this was the city jail until 1959. In John Steinbeck's *Tortilla Flat,* for Big Joe, the Old Monterey Jail was a second home.

U.S. Army Museum

The Presidio. Monterey. (408) 242-8414. Thursday–Monday 9–12:30 and 1:30–4. Free.

This Army-run museum displays the history of old Fort Hill from the Ohlone Indian period to the present. Monuments to Comdr. John Drake Sloat and Fr. Junipero Serra adjoin the museum. Ten history sites are located nearby, among them Rumsen village sites and a ceremonial rock, Father Serra's landing place, and the ruins of the first American fort in Monterey. The museum collection includes uniforms from the turn of the century, saddles, swords, sabers, and other Army equipment, and dioramas of early forts and the first Presidio.

Pacific Grove Museum of Natural History

Forest and Central avenues, Pacific Grove. (408) 372-4212. Tuesday–Sunday 10–5. Closed major holidays. Group tours by appointment. W. Free.

Each October, thousands of Monarch butterflies arrive in Pacific Grove to winter in a grove of pine trees until March. Visitors who arrive in other months can see a marvelous exhibit of the Monarch in this beautifully designed museum. There is also a large collection of tropical and other California butterflies as well as sea otters, fish, mammals, rodents, insects, and birds, stuffed and in photos. The skeleton of a sea otter playing with a clam shell is touching. The life of the Costanoan Indian is revealed in an archaeological "dig." Dioramas and an amazing relief map of Monterey Bay are also worth a look—if the youngsters can tear themselves away from the whale in front. Films.

Second graders get face to face with the whale sculpture at the Pacific Grove Museum of Natural History.

Point Pinos Lighthouse
Off Seventeen-Mile Drive, Pacific Grove. Information at Pacific Grove Museum: (408) 372-4212. Weekends 1–4. Free.

The oldest working lighthouse (1855) on the West Coast, Point Pinos, "Point of Pines," was named by explorer Sebastian Viscaino in 1602. It overlooks the meadows and sand dunes of a golf course on one side, and the whitecapped ocean on the other. A small U.S. Coast Guard maritime museum is open to the public.

The short distance to town along scenic Oceanview Boulevard offers many beautiful sights. Along the way you'll pass Lovers Point, with its marine gardens and tree-shaded picnic grounds.

Mission San Carlos Borromeo
Rio Road, off Highway 1, Carmel. (408) 624-3600. Monday–Saturday 9:30–4:30, Sunday and holidays 10:30–4:30. Donation.

The lovely mission church and cemetery, three museums, and the adobe home of the pioneer Munras family combine to make this mission a "must stop." Fr. Junipero Serra rests in the church, and in the cemetery lies Old Gabriel, 119 years old, baptized by Father Serra. A small museum in the garden houses pictures of the original mission and its restoration. There are Indian grinding pots, arrowheads, baskets, beads, and toys. The long main museum offers fine art from the original mission and a replica of the stark cell Father Serra died in. You'll also find California's first library here: Father Serra's books, bibles, travel commentaries, and technical works. Altarpieces, saddles, the furnished kitchen and dining room, a "clacker" used instead of a bell, and a fabulous new nativity crèche are also of interest, as are mementos of Pope Paul's visit in 1987.

Casa Munras is now a memorial to the Munras family. Visitors can see the keys from the original adobe, family pictures, music and provision boxes, a doctor's bag, jewelry, dresses, and a totally furnished living room.

Carmel

A visit to the Monterey Peninsula is not complete without an hour or two of browsing in the picturesque village of Carmel. The Pine Inn block, bounded by Ocean Avenue, Lincoln, Monte Verde, and Sixth Avenue, is bustling with Victorian shops, gardens, and restaurants. Of particular interest to youngsters are the Gallery of Fine Comic Art (Seventh and Mission; (624-3278), Gepetto's Workshop (Dolores between Ocean and Seventh; 625-1468), and the Brass Rubbing Centre (Mission and Eighth, upstairs; 624-2990). The Mediterranean Market at Ocean and Mission supplies picnic goodies for your walk on Carmel Beach, at the end of Ocean Avenue.

Tor House
26304 Ocean View Avenue, Carmel. (408) 624-1813. One-hour tours on Friday and Saturday by reservation. Adults $5, $3.50 for college students, $1.50 for high school students.

Mature budding poets will enjoy a visit to the home of California poet Robinson Jeffers on a high bluff overlooking the Pacific. Part English country cottage, part stone monument to the mystery of the human imagination, Tor House celebrates the nature around it. Jeffers himself built the low main cottage of stone, with memorabilia from his world travels embedded in the walls, and the 40-foot Hawk Tower that looks like a castle turret. He also built a wonderful "dungeon playroom" for his sons.

Point Lobos State Reserve
Route 1 south of Carmel. (408) 624-4909. Daily 9–5 in winter, later in summer. Cars $3; $2 for senior citizens.

Early Spanish explorers named this rocky, surf-swept point of land Punta de Los Lobos Marinos, or "Point of the Sea Wolves." You can still hear the loud barking of the sea lions and see them on offshore rocks. Point Lobos is an outdoor museum: each tree, plant, and shrub is protected by law, as are the cormorants, pelicans, otters, squirrels, and black-tailed mule deer that live here. One of the last natural stands of Monterey cypress is also found at the reserve. Picnic areas and hiking trails abound.

Thunderbird Book Shop and Restaurant
The Barnyard, off Route 1, Carmel Valley. (408) 624-1803.

The Thunderbird is the kind of bookstore you may have dreamed of: a place where browsing is welcome and the selection of books is extensive. One corner of the store is an informal restaurant. And you can keep browsing as you nosh. The children's book section is now a whole store unto itself.

The Steinbeck House
132 Central Avenue, Salinas. Reservations: (408) 424-2735. Group house tours by appointment. Free.

John Steinbeck's childhood Victorian home is now a lunch restaurant with seatings at 11:45 or 1:15, Monday through Friday. The refurbished home, where Steinbeck wrote *The Red Pony* and *Tortilla Flat,* offers the fresh produce of the Valley amid Steinbeck memorabilia. The Best Cellar basement shop features Steinbeck's books. Profits go to Salinas Valley charities.

    The Steinbeck Library at 110 West San Luis (408-758-7311) displays an extensive collection of John Steinbeck's memorabilia, including reviews, personal correspondence, and a life-sized bronze statue.

The Allen Memorial Cypress Grove looking at Big Dome across Cypress Cove is one of the natural wonders at Point Lobos.

The First Mayor's House

238 East Romie Lane, Salinas. (408) 757-8085. First Sunday of the month, 1–4. Free.

Built in 1868 by Isaac Harvey, the first mayor of Salinas, of redwood lumber hauled from Moss Landing, the cottage has been moved to its present location.

The Boronda Adobe

Boronda Road at West Laurel Drive, Salinas. (408) 757-8085. Weekends 1–4 and by appointment. Free.

Jose Eusebio Boronda's unaltered rancho, built in 1844, is now a museum proudly showing many of its original furnishings.

Issei Pioneer Museum

14 California Street, Salinas. (408) 424-4105. By appointment. Free.

The first and only Issei pioneer museum in the United States, housed in the annex of a Buddhist temple, contains over 600 items donated by *Issei*— the first generation of Japanese to emigrate to the United States—and their descendants. Many of the articles were handmade by the Issei during World II in Arizona and California relocation camps. The oldest item is a book about Tokyo, printed in 1850.

Mission Nuestra Senora De La Soledad

36641 Fort Romie Road, Highway 101 southwest of Soledad. Take the Arroyo Seco off-ramp, then turn right on Fort Romie Road. (408) 678-2586. Wednesday–Monday 10–4. Free.

Founded in 1791 as the 13th in the chain of 21 California missions, this mission dedicated to Holy Mary, Our Lady of Solitude, was in ruins by 1859. Volunteers have restored it to a lovely oasis surrounded by gardens. Visitors may visit the museum and chapel and then spend time in the gift shop, cemetery, and picnic area.

San Antonio de Padua Mission

On Fort Hunter Liggett, off Highway 101 from King City or Bradley, Jolon. (408) 385-4478. Daily 9–4:30. Donation.

San Antonio de Padua is one of the finest of the missions. It was the third mission founded by Fr. Junipero Serra, in 1771. Surrounded by a military base, its natural setting has been preserved, and to visit it is to feel that you're discovering the days of the padres and the Salinan Indians of 200 years ago. Inside the mission museum, on a self-guided tour, you'll see artifacts from mission days, tools for candlemaking, carpentry, wine making, and other old-time skills needed to run a working mission. The gristmill, the aqueduct system, waterwheel, and wine vat stand as the Indians saw them when San Antonio was at its height. The wildflower season in late April and early May is gorgeous, and the annual Fiesta Bar-B-Q is held on the second Sunday of June, close to the Feast of St. Anthony. Steinbeck described the mission when it was in a state of abandonment, in *To a God Unknown*. Today it is a working parish and retreat, served by the Franciscan friars of California.

Public Relations Tours

☐ **Stone Container Corporation** *1078 Merrill, Salinas. (408) 414-1831. November–April, by appointment for children over 10. Free.* Visitors see the manufacturing of corrugated boxes and paper laminations.

☐ **Monterey Peninsula Herald Newspaper** *Pacific and Jefferson streets, Monterey. (408) 372-3311.* Press room and editorial department tours by appointment. Free.

Heading North

Napa, Sonoma, and Lake Counties

The Napa-Sonoma area is best known for the vineyards that grow on its rolling hills and in the Valley of the Moon. But the country itself is welcoming and best seen from the hot air balloons, gliders, planes, and parachutes now available for the brave of heart. Wineries can be fun for youngsters to visit, not only because the wine-making process is fascinating, but because the wine industry is part of California's history and culture. In most wineries, your tour will follow the direction the grape takes, from delivery from the vineyards, to the crushing, to the aging vat, to the bottles in the tasting rooms. The listed wineries offer the most interesting plants and tours, all of which are free (including the tasting, which may include grape juice or nonalcoholic wine). We suggest that you stop at the Napa Valley Olive Oil Manufactory, in St. Helena, or the Oakville Grocery for a loaf of bread and a wedge of cheese to nibble on between tastes.

The Bear Flag Monument in the Old Plaza at Sonoma commemorates the raising of the Bear Flag on the night of June 14, 1846, when California seceded from Mexico before its acquisition by the United States.

Yountville-Vintage 1870
Highway 29, Yountville. (707) 944-2788. Daily 10–5.

This lovely old former winery is part of the original land grant made to Salvador Vallejo in 1838 and was bought in 1870 for $250 in U.S. gold coin. The brick exterior of the building hasn't changed much, but the interior is now a charming complex of shops, theaters, candle and candy makers, potters, a glass blower, and a leather craftsman, who work in open stores.

Robert Mondavi Winery
Highway 29, Oakville. (707) 963-9611. Daily 10:30–4:30. W. Free.

Beautifully designed and landscaped by Cliff May, who designed the *Sunset* magazine building. In addition to tours, the Mondavi Winery offers jazz concerts and special events on summer Sundays in the center lawn.

The Silverado Museum
1490 Library Lane, St. Helena, one block behind Highway 29, Main Street. (707) 963-3757. Tuesday–Sunday 12–4. Closed holidays. Groups by appointment. W. Free.

Robert Louis Stevenson has been associated with the Napa Valley ever since he honeymooned in an abandoned bunkhouse of the Silverado Mine on Mount St. Helena. Today, anyone who grew up on *A Child's Garden of Verses* or *Treasure Island* will appreciate this tribute to the man who wrote them. Portraits of Stevenson abound, including one showing him as a young boy with long flowing curls. Original manuscripts and illustrations; Stevenson's toy lead soldiers, tea set, doll, chess set, and cigarette holder; Henry James's gloves; and memorabilia from Stevenson's plantation in Samoa are neatly displayed in this cheerful museum.

The Christian Brothers/Greystone Cellars
2555 Main Street, St. Helena. (707) 967-3112. Daily 10–4. Free.

Greystone Cellars is the visitors' center of the Christian Brothers. It is the largest stone winery in the country, with more than two acres of floor space and two-foot-thick walls. Brother Timothy's corkscrew collection is on view in the display area. Free tours are conducted every 30 minutes in the summer (no reservations necessary). For one of the thrice-daily barrel tastings, reserve in advance.

Freemark Abbey
Highway 29, above St. Helena. (707) 963-7211. Winery tours daily at 2. Shops open 10–5:30 daily.

The old Freemark Abbey Winery also houses the Hurd Beeswax Candle Factory along with a winery, a restaurant, and a gourmet gift shop. Weekday visitors may see candles being made by hand from 8 to 4:30. And all youngsters will be intrigued by the wooden shutter on the far wall of the inside showroom. It opens to reveal the back of a beehive full of bees filling their honeycomb.

Sterling Vineyards
1111 Dunaweal Lane, off Highway 29, Calistoga. (707) 942-5151. Daily, except holidays, 10:30–4:30. $5 tram fare. Children under 16 free.

An aerial tram ride takes visitors high into the hills to see elevated viewing galleries, lulled by the sound of antique English bells ringing the quarter hour and water falling from sculptured fountains.

Sharpsteen Museum and Sam Brannan Cottage
1311 Washington Street, Calistoga (Highway 29 to Calistoga, right on Lincoln to Washington). (707) 942-5911. Daily 12–4 in winter, 10–4 in summer, and by appointment. W. Free.

This museum, given to the city of Calistoga by Ben Sharpsteen, a Disney Studios artist, is dedicated to the preservation and presentation of the history of Calistoga. Calistoga's pioneer history comes alive in the scale-model dioramas and show boxes. The diorama-mural, *Saratoga of the West,* covers one wall. Other dioramas depict Robert Louis Stevenson, the railroad depot, the Chinese settlement, etc. Sam Brannan, the founder of Calistoga and the first California millionaire, is present in spirit. One of his cottages has been moved to the site, restored, and furnished authentically, a delight for children and adults.

Old Faithful Geyser of California

1299 Tubbs Lane, 2 miles north of Calistoga. (707) 942-6463. Open 9–6 in summer, until 5 in winter. Picnic tables available. Adults $2.50; children 6–12, $1. Group rates.

One of the three "faithful" geysers in the world, Old Faithful erupts approximately every 40 minutes, shooting forth a plume of boiling water and steam 60 feet high. As one little girl exclaimed, when she viewed the geyser after dark: "Look, Mommy, the geyser is washing the stars."

Petrified Forest

Petrified Forest Road, between Calistoga and Santa Rosa. (707) 942-6667. Daily 10–5, until 6 in summer. Adults $3; children 4–11, $1.

Volcanic eruptions of Mount St. Helena six million years ago formed this forest of petrified redwoods, discovered in 1870 and written about by Robert Louis Stevenson. A lovely forest trail passes a 300-foot-long "Monarch" tunnel tree and "the Queen," which was already 3,000 years old when it was buried. On the way out, you'll walk through a specimen shop of fossils and petrified worms, snails, clams, nuts, and wood.

Air Play

The rolling hills and soft wind currents of the area have made the skies here especially accessible. For those who are adventurous, try the following—and check the local Yellow Pages for others. Since companies open and fade with the wind, call for schedules and prices.

□ **Calistoga Soaring Center.** *11546 Lincoln Avenue, Calistoga. (707) 942-5592.* Glider rides, instruction, and rental.

□ **Once in a Lifetime.** *Napa Valley. (800) 722-6665.* Champagne balloon rides.

□ **Balloon Aviation of Napa Valley.** *299 Third Avenue, Napa. (707) 252-7067.*

□ **Balloons Above the Valley.** *1800A Soscal Avenue, Napa. (800) 233-7681/ (707) 253-2222.*

*Like clockwork, Old Faithful bubbles,
then spurts.*

□ **Adventures Aloft.** *P.O. Box 2500, Yountville, CA 94599. (707) 255-8688.*
Flights take off from Vintage 1870 after a 6 a.m. breakfast reception.

☐ **Napa Valley Balloons, Incorporated.** *P.O. Box 2860, Yountville, CA 94599. (800) 253-2244/(707) 253-2224.*

Those seeking more down-to-earth pleasures may choose to Whale Watch on the ocean. **New Sea Angler and Jaws** heads out from Bodega Bay twice a day on weekends and holidays, December 28 through April. Call (707) 875-34995 or write P.O. Box 1148, Bodega Bay, CA 94923.

Petaluma Adobe

3325 Adobe Road, Petaluma (east of Highway 101). (707) 726-4871. Daily 10–5. Tickets usable at all state parks that day: Adults $1, children 50¢. Picnic areas.

Gen. Mariano G. Vallejo's ranch house, Rancho Petaluma, was built in 1836 as the centerpiece of a Mexican land grant of 66,000 acres. Here we learned that in Spanish, *adobe* means "to mix," and that the thick, naturally insulating bricks were made from clay mixed with water and straw and then dried in the sun. A self-guided tour takes you into the kitchen, workshop, candle room, weaving room, servants' quarters, and the Vallejo's upstairs living quarters, graciously furnished with authentic pieces. Outside, there are huge iron cauldrons, clay ovens, a covered wagon, and the racks on which cowhides, the currency of the period, were stretched out to dry. Farm animals add authentic background sounds. On summer weekends, kids can help bake bread in the beehive ovens or take part in the dipping of candles. At one time, General Vallejo had 1,000 workers on the ranch, and it's not hard, standing on the second-floor porch of Rancho Petaluma, to imagine the bustle of yesteryear.

In downtown Petaluma, dubbed in 1918 "The Egg Basket of the World," the **Petaluma Historical Library-Museum** (20 Fourth Street; 778-4398; Thursday–Monday 11–4; free) has rotating and permanent displays such as one on the local poultry industry and another on river history. The bust of Chief Solano, photos of General Vallejo, the Knickerbocker No. 5 fire engine, and the period rooms—especially the one filled with old toys—are popular.

School groups can schedule a "living history overnight," living just as they could have on General Mariano Vallejo's early California rancho during the mid-1800s. They can try their hand at candle dipping, butter churning, and adobe-brick making. Or they can watch costumed craftspeople weave, spin, work on wood and metal, and make lace.

California Coop Creamery.

711 Western Street, at Baker, Petaluma. (707) 778-1234. Groups by appointment. Free.

The retail outlet of a creamery cooperative that has worked together since 1913, offers daily 30-minute tours and a slide show to display how cheese and butter are made. Samples.

Marin French Cheese Company

Petaluma-Pt. Reyes Road, ¼ mile south of Novato Boulevard (707) 762-6001. Daily 10–4. Student programs. Free.

Situated next to a pond in the rolling, cow-speckled hills between Novato and the coast, this is a perfect destination for an afternoon outing or picnic.

The Mouse welcomes visitors to The Creamery cheese factory tour.

own smell. Picnic tables are available, where you can sit and eat a picnic lunch bought on the spot.

Winner's Circle Ranch

5911 Lakeville Highway, Petaluma. Five miles off Highway 101 on the road to Highway 37. (707) 762-1808. Wednesday–Sunday June through October, and by appointment. Showtimes 11 a.m. and 2 p.m. Adults $5, children under 12 and seniors $3. Group rates available.

Winner's Circle Ranch breeds, boards, and trains show-quality miniature horses, which must be no taller than 34 inches. On Horse Tour days, visitors can see mothers and new tiny babies, watch driving exhibitions and video tapes, and have rides in a perfectly proportioned buckboard or Victorian wagon. The trophy room is a magnet for young riders. Picnic areas are available for rent or general use.

It's easy to adore a miniature horse!

Sonoma County Farm Trails

Drive from a mushroom farm and eggery in Petaluma to apple farms in
Sebastopol, turkey growers, or Christmas tree farms. The map lists Farm
Trail members and has a handy product reference guide.

Local favorites are **Krout's Pheasant Farm** (3234 Skillman Lane,
Petaluma; 707-762-8613; Tuesday–Saturday, September 15–January 1),
which has thousands of pheasants, guinea hens, and turkeys, dressed and
live, and **Pet-a-Llama Ranch** (5505 Lone Pine Road, Sebastopol; 707-823-
9394; 10–4 most weekends and by appointment, call after 4 p.m.), where
you can pet llamas, large and small, and see spinning and weaving
demonstrations.

For a copy of the Farm Trails map, send a stamped, self-addressed
envelope to P. O. Box 6032, Santa Rosa, CA 95406.

Sonoma State Historical Park
*From Third Street West and down West Spain Street, past the Plaza to Third
Street East. (707) 938-4779. Daily 10–5. Tickets usable at all state parks
that day. Adults $1, children 50¢. W.*

Lachryma Montis, at Third Street West, named after Tear of the Mountain, the clear spring behind the house, was General Vallejo's city home. Furnished precisely as it was when he lived there with his family, right down to the photograph of Abraham Lincoln in the hall, the house feels as if Vallejo just stepped out for a moment. One daughter's painting is on a wall, along with family photos. Behind the house is the kitchen building and the Chinese cook's quarters. The Chalet in front was once the storehouse and is now a Vallejo museum, containing his books, pictures, saddles, coach, and cattle brand, various remembrances of his family, and biographies of ten of his 16 children.

On the Plaza, you'll walk by Vallejo's first home in Sonoma. Destroyed by a fire in 1867, only the Indian servants' wing survives. There's a small Indian exhibit in the ranger's building. Next, the **Toscano Hotel,** built in 1858, is a carefully restored mining hotel with cards and whiskey glasses still on the tables waiting for the card players to return (tours 1–4 weekends and 11–1 Mondays).

The Mission San Francisco Solano was the northernmost and last of the 21 Franciscan missions in California and the only one established under Mexican, rather than Spanish, rule in 1823. The padres' quarters is the oldest structure in Sonoma. Visitors can walk through the building, looking at interesting exhibits, furnished rooms of the padres, spurs and leggings of the *vaqueros,* and other interesting artifacts of mission life,

Visiting General Vallejo's city house is like stepping backwards in time.

including the primitively painted chapel. A *ramada* has been constructed in the garden for blacksmith, weaving, bread baking, and other period crafts demonstrations. Children can help bake bread on weekends.

In the reconstructed **Soldiers Barracks** (built in 1836), there are exhibits representative of Sonoma history, an audiovisual show, and other activities on weekends.

During your wanderings you may want to stop in at the **Sonoma Cheese Factory** (2 Spain Street; 707-938-5225; 9–6 daily), to see a slide show and young men pounding cheese bags into Sonoma jack. Pick up a picnic, which you can then enjoy in the park across the street.

Buena Vista Winery
One mile out of town, off East Napa Road on Old Winery Road, Sonoma. (707) 938-8504. Daily 10–5. Free.

Buena Vista was the first premium winery in California. Founded in 1857 by the Hungarian count Agoston Haraszthy, who first imported European grape varieties for commercial use, Buena Vista winery is now a California historical landmark. The self-guided tour in the hand-dug limestone caves is wonderfully atmospheric. An art gallery and picnic tables are on the grounds.

Traintown
Broadway, on the main road into Sonoma from San Francisco. (707) 938-3912. Daily in summer and winter weekends, 10:30–5:30. Adults $2.30, children $1.80.

A 20-minute trip on the Sonoma Steam Railroad, a quarter-size reproduction of a mountain-division steam railroad of the 1890s, takes you over trestles, past trees, lakes, tunnels, and bridges and into Traintown. While the train takes on water in Lakeview, you can look through the quarter-sized miniature mining town while listening to its recorded history. The ducks are normal size, but you still feel like Gulliver in the land of Lilliputians.

Jack London State Historic Park
Glen Ellen. (707) 938-5216. Museum open daily 10–5, grounds 8–sunset. $3 per car for the museum and the enlarged park. Picnic areas.

Charmian London built the House of Happy Walls, the finest tribute to a writer in California, as a memorial to her husband. Furnished with the furniture and art gathered for Wolf House, which burned before the Londons could move into it, this museum covers the life of the adventurous young novelist. Once a sailor, prospector, and roustabout, London struggled to gain acceptance as a writer—and you can see a collection of his rejection slips. Photos of the *Snark,* in which the Londons sailed the South Pacific, and treasures collected on their voyages line the walls. Books sold by the rangers are stamped with London's signature, using the stamp he used to save time. London was also an experimental farmer, and the 803 acres of his Beauty Ranch have been purchased by the state. Here you'll see the cottage where he did his writing, concrete silos, the distillery, the stallion barn, the log bathhouse, and the blacksmith's shop. A trail still leads to the Wolf House ruins and to London's grave.

Sonoma County Museum
425 Seventh Street, Santa Rosa, just off HIghway 101. (707) 579-1500. Wednesday–Sunday 11–4. Free.

The Sonoma County Museum, located in a beautifully restored 1910 Post Office building, preserves and honors the rich heritage of Sonoma County. Exhibits change and cover a wide spectrum in both time and subject from Native Americans through Victorian times to today. Cultural vignettes, special exhibits for children, and the Hart Collection of California landscape art also make the museum worth a visit.

The nearby **Codding Museum of Natural History** at 557 Summerfield Road 707-539-0556; Wednesday–Sunday 11–4; free) focuses on local, regional, and worldwide natural history.

The Church of One Tree/Robert L. Ripley Museum
492 Sonoma Avenue, Julliard Park at Santa Rosa Avenue, Santa Rosa. (707) 576-5233. March–October, Wednesday–Sunday 11–4. Adults $1; children 7–17, 50¢; seniors 75¢.

Nestled in tall redwoods, this little church, built from one tree, houses personal articles and drawings of the Believe-It-Or-Not man. A wax figure of Ripley looks out at photos of him with Will Rogers and Shirley Temple, and newspaper clippings as well as samplings of the curiosities he collected.

You might hear some of the "Believe-It-Or-Not" radio shows if the guard has time to play them for you.

Jesse Peter Memorial Museum

Santa Rosa Junior College, 1501 Mendocino Avenue, Santa Rosa. (707) 527-4479. Weekdays, 12–4 and by appointment. Closed holidays and school vacations. Parking behind Bailey Field and at main entrance. Call for events schedule. Free.

Native American arts are celebrated in this tiny bustling center. Southwest pottery, California basketry, Plains beadwork, Northwest Coast art, sculpture, a Klamath River dugout canoe, and grinding stones are part of a continuing exhibit. There are three permanent house models: a Pomo Round House, a Klamath River "Xonta," and a Southwest pueblo. Tours include hands-on activities such as grinding acorns, Indian gambling games, and pump drills. Native American drum and dance groups and Native American arts and crafts sales and demonstrations are scheduled regularly. What child wouldn't enjoy face painting or a traditional story-telling session?

Windsor Waterworks and Slides

8225 Conde Lane, next to Highway 101, 6 miles north of Santa Rosa at Windsor. (707) 838-7360. May–October, 10 a.m.–dusk. All day weekdays: $9 adults, $8 for children 12 and under; weekends $10 and $9. Slide Ride $3 per half hour. Pool and grounds only: $3.50 per day for adults, $2.50 for children 12 and under. Group discounts; events such as birthday parties and exclusive use of the park after Labor Day are encouraged.

Imagine lying down on a foam rubber mat, taking off down a 42-foot drop, speeding 400 feet through tunnels, around spirals and up and over slips— and finally landing in a pool. This adventure in family parks offers four separate water slides, picnic grounds, a large swimming pool, Ping-Pong, horseshoe pits, a wading pool, an electronic game room, and even a softball diamond.

World of Miniatures

Call Windsor information for schedule and prices.

This land of make-believe, a Victorian city with houses, hotels, stores, and an amusement park with a working train and a carousel, and a Hall of Rooms ranging from Paul Revere's drawing room to a modern fantasy bedroom—all done on a one-inch scale, used to be in San Jose. It opened, after we went to press, on Conde Lane in Windsor. A play area and model boat pond will be on the grounds, along with picnic areas.

Healdsburg Museum
132 Matheson Street, Healdsburg. (707) 431-3325. Tuesday–Saturday 12–5. Free.

Fine examples of Pomo Indian basketry and crafts, antique firearms, and 19th-century costumes and tools combine with collections of the town newspapers dating back to 1878 and over 5,000 original historic photographs to make this a worthwhile visit.

Canoe Trips on the Russian River
W. C. "Bob" Trowbridge, 20 Healdsburg Avenue, Healdsburg, CA 95448. (707) 433-7247. Thirty-two dollars per canoe. Over 6 years of age only. Reservations suggested. Call or write for information on trips on the American, Sacramento and Colorado rivers.

The picturesque, winding Russian River is perfect for family canoe trips. It's safe and lovely but can also be fast enough to be exciting. One- and two-hour, and half-day trips are available, and there's a chicken barbecue on weekends in summer. Swimmers only!

The Winery at Asti
26150 Asti Road, Asti exit, Highway 101. (707) 433-2333. Daily 10–5 in summer, closed Monday and Tuesday in winter. Tours, gift shop, picnic area, group functions. W. Free.

Founded in 1881, the Winery at Asti, once Italian Swiss Colony, nestles in a village called Asti because its climate and terrain is like that of Asti in Northern Italy.

Union Hotel Restaurant

Occidental's main street. (707) 874-3555. Lunch: Monday–Saturday 11:30–1:30, $5–$7. Dinners: Monday–Saturday 2–9; Sundays and holidays, 12–8, $6–$13. Mangia!

Dining at the Union Hotel, which has been in business since 1879, is more than just a meal, it's an experience: Italian meals served family style on a plastic red-checked tablecloth with more food than you can possibly eat. One dinner consisted of salami and cheese, beans vinaigrette, salad, lentil soup, zucchini fritters, ravioli, vegetables, your choice of chicken, duck, or steak, good sourdough bread and butter, potatoes, and side dishes. The price? $8 to $11. But one person in your party could simply order soup and salad or just the pasta dinner, and you'd still have a doggy bag for to-morrow's lunch. A half-price child's dinner is available. The frequent waits are made bearable by the game room or a walk through the main street of the town.

Cloverdale Historical Society Museum

215 North Cloverdale Boulevard, Cloverdale. (707) 894-2067. Monday to Friday 9–3:30, and by appointment. (Call (707) 894-2246).

A charming collection of Victoriana snuggles in this 1870 Victorian brick house lacy with gingerbread and a picket fence. The butter churns and tins in the general store and the doll collection on the bedroom look right at home.

Duncan Mills Depot Museum

Highway 116/Moscow Road, 4 miles from the ocean, Duncan Mills. (707) 865-2573. Saturday 10–3. Free.

The only remaining depot of the North Pacific Coast Railroad, which ran the Sausalito-Cazadero route from 1877 to 1935, is now a small museum of railroad history. Tools, telegraph keys, bottles, photos, books, and various vestiges of the logging railway may be seen. Duncan Mills is a growing outpost, with food and gift stores in Victorian style.

Fort Ross State Historic Park

Highway 1, twelve curving miles north of Jenner. (707) 847-3246. Daily 10–4:30. Cars $3 (seniors $2). Free audio wands for self-guided tours. Guided tours available.

California history seems especially romantic in this scenic spot. Fifty-nine buildings, nine of which are inside the redwood walls of the fort, are being rebuilt in a major state restoration project. The Russian Chapel, with a bell you can ring in front, is as spare and quiet as it was when the fort was sold to John Sutter in 1841. Visitors can climb up into the eight-sided blockade tower and seven-sided blockhouse to look out over the little beach and inlet where Russian fur merchants used to trade with the Indians. The commandant's house serves as a small museum, with a Russian samovar, an Aleut kayak, and artifacts found on the grounds. Don't forget to toss a penny into the wishing well!

Visitors at Fort Ross can pretend they're on a Czarist Russian outpost, walking through the stockade, commandant's house, guest house, blockhouses, and the first Russian Orthodox chapel built in North America. This is the deep "russian well" built to secure water if the fort came under siege.

Living history pageants sponsored by the State Parks Association help bring the past to life at Fort Ross. A picnic grounds adjoins the Fort.

Lake County Museum

Old Courthouse, 255 North Main Street, Lakeport. (707) 263-4555. Wednesday–Saturday 10–3:45 in winter; also open Sunday 11–3:45, May– September. Free.

Beautifully woven Pomo baskets and hunting traps are nicely displayed in this country museum, along with arrowheads, spears, and small tools. Firearms used to tame the west, such as the Kentucky long rifle and the Slotterbeck, made in Lakeport in the late 1800s, are also intriguing. Other displays include turn-of-the-century clothing and household items and samples of the semiprecious gems and minerals found in Lake County. Did you know that the Lake County Diamond, a natural or faceted quartz crystal, could be either pink or lavender? The museum is also the home of Lake County Genealogical Society, which boasts hundreds of books to help you find your roots.

Skindivers, rockhounds, and budding marine biologists enjoy exploring the Sonoma coast. This is Salt Point State Park, north of Fort Ross.

Redwood Country: Mendocino, Humboldt, and Del Norte Counties

Redwood country is one of the most beautiful areas in America. Stately redwoods line the roads "as far as the fog flows," and the Pacific Ocean

Boats come and go and youngsters fish for shiners at Noyo, a salmon port south of Ft. Bragg on the rugged Mendocino Coast.

crashes into the shoreline. Some of the beaches are craggy and surrounded by dangerous currents. Others are calm and protected, with long empty stretches just made for solitary walks.

You can dash up from San Francisco on Highway 101 or you can spend hours winding along the coastline on Highway 1. You can enjoy the Victoriana of Ferndale and Eureka, or you can lose yourself in the tiny fishing villages of Rockport and Noyo. Whale watching is a popular pastime from December to April. The waters may be too cold to swim in, but the fish thrive and are there for the catching.

You can get away from it all in the sylvan glens along the Avenue of the Giants, marveling at your smallness next to a 300-foot tree. To show the aims, methods, and benefits of industrial forest management within the redwood region, several firms have made demonstration forests available to the public. Tours are self-guided, and there are restrooms and picnic areas available. You'll learn that only 1 percent of the tree is living: the tips of its roots, the leaves, buds, flowers, seed, and a single thin layer of cells sheathing the tree. You'll see Douglas firs, white firs, and redwood residuals— redwood trees that have sprung up from seeds and sprouts. You'll find the forests along Highway 128, on new and old Highway 101, and on Highway 299.

Redwood country lets you set your own pace—there are many places to see and things to do close to each other, and there are enough parks and beaches for you to relax or picnic in, whenever the mood strikes. It's a great getaway for a weekend or a week.

Mendocino

Once an old lumber port, settled in 1852, Mendocino is now a mecca for driftwood collectors, artists, and tourists. The town has appeared in many movies, and there are interesting little streets to browse along when it gets too foggy for beachcombing. Among the highlights are *The Mendocino Art Center* (540 Lake Street; daily 10–5; special movies and shows at night; 707-937-5819); *The Mendocino Ice Cream Company* on Main (937-5844); *Sky's No Limit,* the kite and Frisbee store on Lansing (937-0173); and *The Joys of Toys* (937-0100). The old Masonic Lodge Hall, at Lansing and Ukiah, with its massive redwood sculpture, *Father Time and the Maiden,* carved from one piece of redwood, is a landmark.

The Kelly House Historical Museum (4500 Albion Street, 957-5791; daily 1–4; donation) is a pleasant step back in time. Drop in, too, at the interpretive center at the *Ford House* on Main Street. The nearby *Temple of Kwan Ti,* one of the first buildings in Mendocino, may be seen by appointment.

Mendocino Coast Botanical Gardens
18220 North Highway 1, 6 miles north of Mendocino. (707) 964-4352. Daily 9–5, April–September; 10–4, October–March. Retail nursery and cafe. Admission $4, seniors $3, student groups and those under 12 free. Group discounts and tours. W.

Seventeen acres of formal gardens, coastal pine forest, fern canyons, and ocean bluff explode with multicolored flowers and teem with protected wildlife, including 60 species of birds. Rhododendrons bloom in April and May; perennials from May to October. Fall is mushroom season, and the heath blooms all winter, when you can see a gray whale migration. Sea lions rest on the rocks. Picnickers are welcome.

Guest House Museum
Main Street, Fort Bragg. (707) 961-2825. Wednesday–Sunday 10–4. Free.

This gift to the city from the Georgia Pacific Company houses historical pictures of the logging industry, a huge bellows, mementos of the loggers, and models of ships. Films and talks contrast logging's industrial present and its rugged past. Be sure to walk to the foot of Redwood Avenue to see the huge slice of redwood that was 1,753 years old in 1843.

Nearby, at the foot of Walnut Street, is the *Georgia Pacific Nursery* (weekdays 9–4, April–November), which holds four million trees. A display room explains reforestation and timber management. An arboretum, nature trails, and picnic tables are available. A free packet of redwood seeds is mailed to each visiting family.

The Skunk Railroad
Skunk Depot, Main and Laurel, Fort Bragg. (707) 964-6371. Reserve by writing to California Western Railroad, P.O. Box 907, Fort Bragg 95437. Half and full-day trips from and to Fort Bragg and Willits to Northspur are available at prices ranging from about $8 for children for a 3-hour trip and $20 for adults for the full day.

The Skunk Railroad, named for the smell the first gas engines used to cast over the countryside, has been making passenger trips from Fort Bragg to Willits since 1911. During the 40-mile trip the train crosses 30 trestles and bridges, goes through two tunnels, twists and turns over spectacularly curved track, and travels from the quiet Noyo riverbed to high mountain passes through redwood forest. The bouncy diesel Skunk is well worth the price and time. If it's summer, try the open observation car.

There's also a train from Willits to Eureka. *The Redwood Coast Railway Co.*, at 299 East Commercial Street, (800) 482-7100, runs along the Eel River through redwood forest to Old Town, 145 miles away. Call for times and prices.

Mendocino County Museum
400 East Commercial Street, Willits. (707) 459-2736. Wednesday–Sunday, 10–4:30. Free.

The Mendocino County Museum is a storehouse of memories, dreams, and hard-won lessons of survival amidst the rugged beauty of California's north

All aboard! for a railroad romp through the redwoods.

coast. Exhibits use local artifacts to celebrate and explain the life and times of Mendocino County. Oral history interviews capture living memories on tape. Collections of Pomo and Yuki baskets represent the vanished ancestors and today's descendants of the region's Native American. The danger and excitement of everyday work in the redwoods is recalled through living history programs featuring restored logging artifacts discovered in the Mendocino woods. Changing exhibits provide fresh experiences for museum visitors.

The Drive-Thru Tree
Old Highway 101, Leggett. (707) 925-6363. Daily 9–5; in summer, 8 a.m. until dark. $2.50 per car.

This large, chandelier-shaped, 315-foot redwood was tunneled in 1934, and a standard-size contemporary car just fits through. It's 21 feet in diameter and, in spite of the tunnel, is still alive. The winding dirt road leading to the tree takes you right to a little gift shop and to the highway. There are 200 acres of nature trails and picnic areas by the side of a lake that is a home to geese. Logging relics are on the grounds. Kids like the log with a hole you can crawl into.

Confusion Hill/Mountain Train Ride
75001 North Highway 101, Piercy. Eighteen miles south of Garberville. (707) 925-6456. Daily 9–6. Confusion Hill: adults $2.50; ages 6–12, $1.25. Mountain train ride: April–September. Adults $2.50; ages 3–12, $1.25.

The miniature Mountain Train follows many switchbacks to take you 1¼ miles up to the summit of a redwood mountain, through a tunnel tree, and back down. Try a different kind of experience at Confusion Hill, a spot where gravity is defied. You seem to be standing sideways; water runs uphill; your friends shrink or grow taller in front of you. Is seeing really believing?

Avenue of the Giants
Humboldt Redwoods State Park, Weott. (707) 946-2311. Day use $3, camping $10 per night.

Standing tall as a nominee for the most spectacular 33 miles anywhere is this bypass road winding leisurely beneath 300-foot trees. One of the few tree species to have survived from the time of the dinosaurs, the redwoods are majestic, awesome trees to behold. You'll drive through a protected wilderness of soaring trees and moss- and fern-carpeted landscape occasionally spotted with deer. Founder's Grove, Rockefeller Forest, and Children's Forest are some of the best of the special groves. The Tree House in Piercy, Hobbiton and the Chimney Tree near Phillipsville, and the Drive-thru Tree in Myers Flat are more commercial stopping places.

Pacific Lumber Company
Scotia, 27 miles south of Eureka. (707) 764-2222. Mill tours year round at 7:30 and 10:30 a.m., 12:30 and 3 p.m., Monday–Thursday; Friday 12:30–2:30. Museum: summer weekdays 10–4. Free.

Scotia is an old logging town that was built entirely of redwood. Entirely owned by Pacific Lumber Company, it is probably the last wholly owned town in the United States. The museum, a fine old mansion, presents pic-

Camping at Jedediah Smith Redwoods State Park, northeast of Crescent City, among redwoods and lush vegetation, can be magical.

tures of the loggers at work and play and a collection of logging equipment, tools, and relics. Here's where you get the pass for the self-guided tour of the mill, which goes up two flights of stairs and takes about 45 minutes. You'll follow the processing of a log from the moment it comes out of the pond. The first step is one of the most impressive: a debarker that uses water pressure to peel the log as if it were a banana. Many things go on all at once in the mill (which can be loud and more unnerving for timid adults than for kids).

The nearby Scotia Fish Rearing Pond, built by the lumber company to help rehabilitate the Eel River, raises 100,000 steelhead and salmon each year.

Depot Museum
Park Street, Fortuna. (707) 725-2495. Daily 12–5 in summer; closed Thursday and Friday, September–May. W. Donation.

The 1893 train depot is now a small museum housing Fortuna memories of loggers, farmers, Indians, and the railroad. The old teletype is at the ready; fancy dresses and shoes wait for the next dance; fishing poles and tackle stand waiting for the fishing trip; and pictures and schoolbooks round out the collection. The three old marriage certificates are lovely. The museum is located in Rohnert Park, a lovely family park with picnic tables and playground equipment. The Depot offers a free map of nearby attractions for the disabled.

Visitors in autumn may want to stop by **Clendenen's Cider Works** (Twelfth Street and Newberg Road; 725-2133) to see the mill in action and buy fresh cider. **Chapman's Gem and Mineral Shop and Museum,** 4 miles south of the city on Highway 101 (725-4732), is open 10–5 daily in summer.

Ferndale Museum
Shaw and Third streets, Ferndale. (707) 786-4466. Tuesday–Saturday 12– 4, Sunday 1–4. Closed Tuesday June–September, closed January. Adults $1; children 16 and under, 50¢, children 6 and under free when accompanied by an adult. Group demonstrations by appointment.

A blacksmith shop with a working forge, antique farming and logging equipment, and a working seismograph are permanent exhibits, along with rotating collections that show the lifestyles, work habits, and activities of Ferndale's ancestors. Since most of the successful businessmen made their money with farms, their Victorian homes were called "butterfat palaces" and the town was called "Cream City." Ferndale, a restored and repainted Victorian town, is a wonderful place to spend time.

Clarke Memorial Museum
Third and E streets, Eureka. (707) 443-1947. Tuesday–Saturday 10–4. W. Free.

This large regional-history museum is housed in a palatial 1912 bank. A recent addition is devoted to the Native American Indian culture of north-western California. The world's largest and most complete collections of Hoopa, Yurok, and Karuk regalia and basketry are at the Clarke, with over 1,200 artifacts displayed. There are also extensive collections on the development of Humboldt County: shipbuilding, logging, milling, firearms, furniture, textiles, and Victorian decorative arts.

The Clarke Museum is located in Eureka's Old Town, the restored district on the shore of Humboldt Bay. This district of Victorian commercial and residential buildings, crowned by the remarkable Carson Mansion (on Second and M, not open to the public), the greatest Victorian in California, includes many bookstores and boutiques. Be sure to visit the shop of the Northern California Indian Development Council on F Street, next to the Bon Bonière Ice Cream Parlor. There's a self-guided tour if you want to see how oysters are processed on the shoreline; call 442-2947.

The M/V Madaket Bay Tour
Sails from the foot of C Street, Eureka. Call (707) 442-9440 for times and prices.

The 75-minute cruise aboard this venerable vessel, a 1910 ferry, takes in oyster beds, pelican roosts, sawmills, an egret rookery, a former Indian village, and includes history of the area.

Sequoia Park Zoo
3414 West Street at Glatt, Eureka. (707) 442-6552. Tuesday–Sunday 10–5, until 7 in summer. Children's Petting Zoo: Tuesday–Sunday 11:30–3:30 in summer. W. Free.

Located in the heart of the redwoods, the Sequoia Park Zoo houses an excellent variety of both local and exotic animals, including the gibbon, otter, emu, prairie dog, reticulated python, black bear, and Pacific giant salamander. The zoo is part of the Sequoia Park, which encompasses picnic areas, a playground, flower gardens, a duck pond, and 54 acres of north coast redwoods.

Fort Humboldt State Historic Park

3431 Fort Avenue off Highway 101, Eureka. (707) 445-6567. Daily 9–5. Free.

High on a windy hill overlooking a shopping mall, Fort Humboldt is primarily an outdoor museum of the logging industry. Old machinery is accompanied by large display boards telling what it was like to be a logger in the 19th century. A logger's cabin is furnished with a stove, a bed, a shelf of beans, and a "pin-up" calendar. You learn how to "fell" a tree (the falling branches are called "widow makers") and then see how it is dragged out of the forest and cut up. One logger notes that it's "a shame to wash clothes

Campsites and hiking trails make enjoying the placid Eel River a pleasure in summer. But in winter, the Eel is torrential, swollen by storms.

while they can still bend." An 1884 Falk locomotive and an 1892 Anersonia locomotive are on view. Old Fort Humboldt, where Ulysses S. Grant served as a staff officer in the 1850s, is nearby.

A short drive away are the only two covered bridges in the area. Take 101 South to Elk River Road and follow along to either Zane or Berta road. The bridges are covered not to protect them from snow but to protect the lumber from rain: boarding them up preserves the wood longer and is less expensive than constant repainting.

Samoa Cookhouse

Samoa Road, Eureka. (707) 442-1659. Breakfast: children 7–11, $3.45; adults $4.55. Lunch: children 3–6, $2.55; children 7–11, $3.55; adults $4.75. Dinner: children 3–6, $3.75; children 7–11, $5.75; adults $8.75.

Family-style meals are served seven days a week in this old lumber-camp cookhouse that was once relief quarters for shipwreck victims. The long tables are set as they were in 1885, with red and white checked cloths and large bottles of catsup. Our breakfast consisted of huge amounts of orange juice, coffee, delicious French toast, and sausage. Dinner the night before included thick cuts of ham and sole, and peach pie with all the fixings. Before or after the meal, wander through the adjoining rooms to see an assemblage of logger's boots, dinner bells, kitchen utensils, and a steam coffeemaker that once served 500 men three times a day.

Humboldt State University Marine Laboratory

Trinidad, off Highway 101 at Edwards and Ewing. (707) 677-3671. Monday–Friday 8–5, Saturday and Sunday 12–5 during school year. W. Free.

Located near Land's End, in the picturesque fishing village of Trinidad, this working laboratory is open to the public for self-guided tours. Hallway aquariums hold rare and common mollusks and crustaceans, and fresh- and saltwater fish. Varicolored anemones, walleye surf perches, Siamese tigerfish, and shovel-nose catfish were there for our visit, along with a tame wolf eel and a small black octopus. Exhibits change regularly. Special school programs.

Stop at the **Trinidad Lighthouse** on your way to the lab. This is the spot where the Spaniards landed on Trinity Sunday in 1775. The original gear system of descending weights still works to turn the light, but the original two-ton bell is for display only.

Patrick's Point State Park, five miles north of the lab along the shore, boasts a small museum of Yurok artifacts and rock displays at park headquarters. There is a $2 admission for each car (707-677-3570; W).

Prairie Creek Redwoods State Park
Highway 101, near Orick. (707) 488-2171. Daily 9–5. Free. Junior ranger programs 5 days a week for children 6–12. call for times and topics. W.

Roosevelt elk roam this state park and can be seen grazing on the meadow outside the Visitors Center. Inside the center you'll see an interesting exhibit on the elk and the trees, ferns, flowers, and animals in the area. The most extraordinary object is a madrone tree that grew to envelope the skull of an elk. Fine nature trails lead from the center. On one is a living redwood that has been hollowed out by fire. Sixty-five schoolchildren have been inside it at one time.

Just south of the park, on 101, is the **Prairie Creek Fish Hatchery** (488-2253; 8–5 daily; free), which raises king and silver salmon and coastal cutthroat and rainbow trout.

Just north of Orick, at Bald Hills Junction, the **Arcata Redwood Company's Mill A** welcomes visitors to view operations from an overhead catwalk. A Forest Renewal Exhibit is five miles farther north. Four miles south on 101, the **Rellim Demonstration Forest** offers a free self-guiding tour (707-464-3144).

Trees of Mystery
Redwood Highway, U.S. 101, 16 miles south of Crescent City, Klamath. (707) 482-5613. Daily 8–7, until 9 in summer; 8–5 daily in winter. Closed holidays. W. Adults $5; seniors $4; children 6–12, $2.50.

A talking 49-foot-tall Paul Bunyan greets you at the entrance, and then you walk through a hollowed redwood log into a forest of redwoods, where recorded music and explanations take you past trees such as the Fallen Giant, the Elephant Tree, and the immense and moving Cathedral Tree. Going back down the hill is our favorite section—Paul Bunyan's Trail of Tall Tales—where you hear how Babe the Blue Ox was found, how the Grand Canyon was dug, and how Sourdough Sam makes his pancakes. (His recipe includes the lard from one summer-fattened bear.) Indians called this "a place of spirits," and the End of the Trail Museum in the gift

A 48-foot-high Paul Bunyan and talking Blue Ox welcome visitors to the "talking trees" at the Trees of Mystery.

shop offers an extensive array of clothes and artifacts of tribes ranging from the Mississippi to the Pacific and north to the Aleutians.

The Drive-Through Tree, five miles south on Highway 101 at the north end of the Klamath River Bridge (known for its decorative golden bears), is worth a short visit.

Undersea World
Highway 101 South, Crescent City. (707) 464-3522. Summer: 9–8 daily; winter: 10–4. Adults $5.95; children 5–12, $3.95. Group rates. School programs.

Over 5,000 marine specimens live in this habitat ten feet below sea level. The ferocious wolf eels, scurrying crabs, sun starfish, and black snappers that stand vertically to aid their digestion are all native to the area and are presented in their natural environments. You'll see sables, big skates, starry

Seaside picnics in Del Norte County, near Crescent City, offer driftwood fantasies along with the sand and crisp salty breezes.

flounders, and California sea lions, too. There's also a touchable tidepool exhibit and exhibits of dangerous sea creatures.

Del Norte Historical Society Museum

577 H Street, Crescent City. (707) 464-3922. Monday–Friday 10–4, Saturday 1–4. Adults $1.50; children under 12, 50¢.

The 1935 version of *The Last of the Mohicans* was filmed in Crescent City, and this museum, once a county jail, has many photos of the Indians who appeared in it. A Yurok bark house and stick games, headdresses, beads, dolls, and baskets of Tolowa, Pomo, Hoopa, and Yurok tribes are shown, as are photos of Crescent City since its beginnings, with lots of before and after shots of the 1964 tidal wave. Unicycles, jail cells, a moonshine still, pioneer clothing, the Frensel lens from the Point St. George lighthouse, and collections belonging to local residents bring new life to local history.

Battery Point Lighthouse
Crescent City. (707) 964-3922. Wednesday–Sunday 10–4, tide permitting, April–September. Adults $1.50; children under 12, 50¢.

Battery Point Lighthouse is located offshore from Crescent City on a little island accessible only at low tide. The original light is still workable, and the old logbook, banjo clock, shipwreck photos, and nautical mementos add to the enjoyment of a visit. Although many may have hopes of being stranded by the tide, the wealth of native plants and the view of the ocean from the tower will make up for any disappointment at being back on the mainland.

Ship Ashore
Smith River, Highway 101, three miles south of the Oregon border. (707) 487-3141. Daily 10–5:30. Free.

This 160-foot former luxury yacht, which also served with the U. S. Navy during World War II, is now a landlocked gift shop with a complete naval and historical museum under the main deck. The wheelhouse is full of ship models—from a seventeenth century Man O'War to a World War II vessel—and kids can take a turn at the wheel itself. An autograph and the address of Nujuo Fujita, the only Japanese pilot to drop a firebomb on the United States, is on the wall. Downstairs you'll find a potpourri of memories and souvenirs that range from a 1910 country doctor's kit to Alaskan boots, stuffed owls and armadillos, an extensive shell collection, shop blueprints, swords and uniforms, clothes and necklaces from the Edward Lopez family of the Tolowa tribe, and a fascinating pirate's den that presents the lore and rules pirates lived by.

Simpson Korbel Forest Nursery
Highway 299 near Blue Lake in Korbel. (707) 822-0371, ext. 539. Free.

Tours by appointment only at 11 a.m. and 1 p.m. in summer.

Fishing at Blue Lake can be peaceful and serene.

Mad River State Fish Hatchery

Blue Lake. (707) 822-0592. Daylight hours. Groups by appointment only. Free.

Salmon and steelhead fish eggs, baby fish, and fingerlings may be seen. By the way, the river is not ferocious. It was named for a fight between Joe Greek and L. K. Wood, two explorers of the region, in 1849.

The Big Valley

Solano, Sacramento and Stockton

Today, the Sacramento area is the political heartland of the state of California. Two hours away from San Francisco, the city of Sacramento is worth a visit to get a feeling for how the world's eighth-largest economy functions.

At different times, the capital of California has been Benicia, Vallejo, and San Jose. The state capitol is now beautifully restored domed building in Sacramento. The rich farmland surrounding the city is reflected in the 40-acre Capital Park in the city, and you will appreciate the mix of urban, suburban, and rural settings that symbolize the variety of California's lifestyles.

Stockton, south of Sacramento, is one of the entrances to the Gold Country. Visitors will find the rolling hills and farmland dotted by small towns. Stockton is named in honor of Commodore Robert Stockton, who led the forces that captured California for the United States in 1847. The lakes and peaceful atmosphere of the San Joaquin Valley add to the ambience of the area, and water-sports lovers will find ample opportunities for houseboating, skiing, fishing, and every kind of boating.

The past meets the present in a
wonderfully restored Old Sacramento.

Marine World Africa USA

Marine World Parkway, Vallejo, off Highway 80. (707) 643-ORCA/644-4000. Wednesday–Sunday and holidays: 9:30–5 in winter, daily until 6 in summer, 7 on weekends. Adults $15.95, over 60, $11.95; children 4–12, $10.95. Dolphin strollers and wheelchairs for rent. Picnic areas. Red and White Ferry from San Francisco's Pier 41, (415) 546-2896. Season tickets and group discounts available.

Dancing dolphins, killer whales, waterskiing extravaganzas, an ecology theater, and a "gentle jungle" petting area are just some of the many attractions in this remarkable theme park and ecology center. When the kids tire of looking at the aquarium and other exhibits, they can sit and watch an exciting show or let off steam at the Whale-of-a-Time Playground. There are elephant and camel rides, animal encounters, seals to feed, and dozens of ways to have a wonderful day.

Vigga, a 10-year-old female killer whale, sprays a mouthful of water onto an unsuspecting volunteer at Marine World's killer whale and dolphin show. But you can't say the people in the front rows weren't warned!

Vallejo Naval and Historical Museum

734 Main Street, Vallejo. (707) 643-0077. Tuesday–Friday 10–4:30, Saturday 1–4:30. Adults 50¢, children 25¢.

Ship models, murals, and the periscope from the U.S.S. *Baya* attract naval buffs to this small but special museum.

Herman Goelitz Candy Co.

2400 North Watney Way, Fairfield. (Off Highway 80 down West Texas to Beck Avenue; right to Courage Drive; right on North Watney.) (707) 428-2380. Store open Monday–Friday 10–5. Video on request. Samples. Tours by reservation. No open-toed shoes. No tank tops or shorts. No children under 6. Shoes with soft soles recommended.

"The day I went to the Jelly Belly factory I fell in love. You could see how they make the candy and how they put the chocolate on the raisins. They

At the Jelly Belly factory, you always have room for one more.

put the raisins in a barrel and the barrel turned. You'll get samples of candy. You will enjoy it. I did. They have jelly beans in 40 flavors which are very good. The Jelly Belly is an interesting place to go and see how candy is made. You should go. You will have a blast." Tina Miranda, Fourth Grade, David A. Weir School, Fairfield.

The Goelitz Candy Co. has been in business since 1898. They invented the jelly bean, after candy corn, in 1926. Gummi bears are a recent addition. An informative video begins the 30-minute tour. (There are only 4 calories per jelly bean—and it takes ten days to make one.)

Vacaville Museum
212 Buck Avenue, downtown Vacaville. (707) 447-4513. Wednesday–Sunday 1–4:30. Adults $1, students 50¢. Wednesdays free. W.

This active museum honors the city's heritage, its founders, and the farmers who settled Solano County. Rotating exhibits such as the Vaca Valley Doll Club's collection and "Victorian Dining" will interest the whole family.

The **Peña Adobe**, on Highway 80 five miles south of Vacaville, is open during the day for visitors who want to see what rancho life was like. The Peña Adobe is the original adobe, built on an ancient Indian site, and some of the Wintu artifacts found during restoration are displayed. There are picnic tables on the grounds.

Lagoon Valley Soaring
Vacaville Gliderport, 5730 Rivera Road, Peña Adobe exit, Highway 80. (800) 345-0905/(707) 447-4500. Open 10–sunset, weather permitting. Gliding and flying rides and lessons. Write P. O. Box 176, Vacaville CA, 95688.

Gliding flights last about 15 glorious silent minutes, or you can go up for a scenic cruise in a 1928 Travelaire biplane or the more spectacular aerobatic ride in the Great Lakes replica biplane.

Yolano Harvest Trails
To receive your map, send a stamped, self-addressed envelope to Yolano Harvest Trails, P. O. Box 484, Winters, CA 95694.

Farmers and farm stores have put together a map and guide to producers open to the public. An afternoon outing to see where our food comes from can be educational as well as entertaining. Youngsters will particularly want to visit **The Babcock Ranch,** where you can pick produce yourself (2434 Morrison Lane, Suisun; 707-864-0440; May–September 9–5); **The Wool Warehouse,** to see sheep and the processing of wool, from carding and spinning to weaving (7 East Main Street, Winters; 916-795-3262; Monday–Saturday 10–3; tours by appointment); and **The Research Farm,** to see an amazing collection of flora and fauna, from llamas to catfish to pussywillows to peacocks to Barbados sheep to sacred lotus plants and comb honey. The farm also has a special program for bringing animals to the classroom (Route 2, Davis; 916-758-1387; by appointment).

The Nut Tree
Monte Vista Avenue, off Highway 80, Vacaville. (707) 448-6411.
Daily 7 a.m.–9p.m.

The Nut Tree is more than a restaurant—it's an enjoyment center. The restaurant is lavishly decorated with rooms facing huge glass aviaries where brilliantly colored birds fly, sing, and eat fruits and seeds. Breakfast, lunch, and dinner prices are moderate, with an emphasis on California fruits and produce. There are some restaurants and snack bars on the grounds, as well as a huge gift store and a toy store. Free mechanical animals, play mirrors, Polynesian tree huts and a funny-face play-wall will entice the children. Outside the toy store, they can board a miniature train for a five-minute ride ($1 each, three for $2.50). The family home of the founders of the Nut Tree is on the grounds and has been completely restored. Tours are available by appointment.

Yolo County Museum
512 Gibson Road, Woodland. Highway 80 to Route 113. (916) 666-1045.
Monday and Tuesday 10–4, weekends 12–4, and by appointment. Free.

Housed in the Southern mansion built by William Gibson to remind him of his Virginia home, this museum records area history as seen through the lives of one family. Each room represents another era and a different generation of Gibsons, from 1850 to 1940. The dairy, root cellar, and washroom outside still work. Antique farm equipment, an herb garden, and picnic areas are on the grounds.

There's another unique place to visit in Woodland, a must-stop for junior mechanics: **The A. W. Hays Truck Museum**, the largest collection of antique trucks in the world. This is a private, personal collection, and it's best to be there when A.W. himself can show you around, so call first (2000 East Main Street; 916-666-1044; weekdays 10–4 and sometimes on weekends; adults $3, teens $1; W).

Old Sacramento

Sacramento was the major transportation hub for north-central California, providing a convenient location where water and land transportation systems could meet. Today, along the Sacramento River where Capt. John Sutter established his embarcadero in 1839, an important part of Sacramento's history has been restored to its former glory. Fifty-three structures built during the Gold Rush stand as living memorials to the past. Inside are restaurants, stores, offices, and museums. For tour information, call (916) 443-7825. Horse and buggy and covered-wagon rides are available.

The **Old Eagle Theater** at Front and J streets, which first opened in 1849, presents old melodramas and plays (box office: 446-6761; tours daily, 10–4; Free).

Central Pacific Passenger Station at Front and J streets (448-4466; 10–5 daily; free with Railroad Museum ticket) is a reconstruction of a station that was built in 1876. Waiting rooms, ticket offices, baggage rooms, and railroad cars tell their stories.

Old Sacramento Schoolhouse at Fort and L looks just as it did in the 1880s (383-2636; Monday–Saturday 9:30–4:30, Sunday 12–4:30; free).

B. F. Hastings Museum at Second and J was the first western terminus of the Pony Express and the Sacramento office of Wells Fargo. The Wells Fargo and Pony Express exhibits beguile, as do the reconstructed Supreme Court rooms, the Grass Valley stage, and posters on the early post office system. You can tap out Morse code or write with a quill pen (445-4655; Tuesday–Sunday 10–5; free).

Huntington-Hopkins Hardware Store, a reconstruction of the west's most historic hardware store, shows off old tools and supplies in a surprisingly appealing display (1111 I Street; 446-4466; Tuesday–Sunday; free).

"Sacramento Illustrated" offers a 15-projector multimedia portrayal of Sacramento's history (925 Front Street; 638-0355; weekends 12–6; a nominal fee is charged).

The Sacramento History Center is an ultramodern portrayal of the Sacramento Valley from prehistoric times to the present. Docents are on hand to explain the exhibits, from the wall of pictures of Yosemite outings to the canning machinery that runs around you as you walk down the stairs (101 I Street; 449-2057; daily 10–5; adults $2.50, children 6–17, $1; seniors $1.50).

California State Railroad Museum

Second and I streets, Old Sacramento. (916) 448-4466. Groups: 445-4209. Daily 10–5. Adults $3; children 6–7, $1. Groups by appointment. W. In summer, there are special hourly steam train excursions from the Central Pacific Freight Depot at Front and K streets. Adults $3; children 6–17, $2.

This state-of-the-art museum combines slide shows, theater presentations, panel exhibits, dioramas, interpretive exhibits, shiny locomotives, and historic railroad cars to walk in and around to see how trains have affected our history and culture. You start your self-guided tour with a movie—and then walk through the back wall of the theater into Gold Rush California. Lucius Beebe's elegant private car, the Railway Post Office Car where you can sort mail, and the St. Hyacinthe Sleeping Car that really rocks are three highlights. Don't forget to see the toy miniature train collection upstairs.

Matthew McKinley Paddlewheel Excursion Boat

1207 Front Street, Sacramento. (916) 441-6482. Call for prices and schedule.

This luxuriously appointed riverboat offers cruises for individuals and groups, from a renovated wharf in Old Sacramento. The cruise goes downstream past Miller Park, the old industrial wharves, and the Sacramento Yacht Club.

Crocker Art Museum

216 O Street at Third, Sacramento. (916) 449-5423. Wednesday–Sunday 10–5, Tuesday 1–9. Closed holidays. Ages 18–64, $2; ages 7–17 and over 65, $1. W. Tours for the hearing or visually impaired.

The oldest art museum in the west was built around 1873 to house the paintings and prints collected by Judge Edwin Bryant Crocker. The collec-

New music and antique instruments amuse at the Family Festival in the Crocker Art Gallery.

tion includes pottery from the fifth century B.C. through contemporary works of art. Rococo mirrors, frescoed ceilings, and curving staircases make the building itself a work of art. Concerts, lectures, and other special demonstrations and events are scheduled throughout the year.

California State Capitol
Tenth and Capitol, Capitol Mall. (916) 445-4209. Daily 9–5. Free. Guided tours on the hour. W.

After 13 years of construction, the State Capitol building was completed in 1874. It has recently been restored to its historic 19th-century dignity and beauty. It's fun to wander the halls and see the state window displays—and hear the rustle of politics in action.

Old Governor's Mansion
1526 H Street at 16th, Sacramento. (916) 323-3047. Daily 10–4, with tours on the hour. Adults $1; children 6–17, 50¢.

The official residence of California's 13 governors from 1903 to 1967 is now a handsome Victorian museum that embodies the history of the state. The mélange of furnishing styles reflects the different inhabitants. The old carriage house has been converted to a museum where you may see hats, fans, parasols, and memorabilia of the governors and their families.

Sutter's Fort State Historic Park
2701 L Street at 28th Street, Sacramento. (916) 445-4422. Daily except holidays, 10–5. Adults $1; children under 18, 50¢. Information wand free. Tours and demonstrations by appointment. W.

Sutter's Fort is one of the best places to relive California history. The fort and its buildings and stables are perfectly reconstructed, and the cooperage, distillery, saddle shop, candle-making room, kitchens, trading post, guardroom, bunk room, and Sutter's family quarters are all as they once were. The songs and information provided through audio wands are clear, helpful, and entertaining. For example, while facing a model of James Marshall showing Sutter the gold he found at the mill, you hear their conversation and Sutter's German-Swiss accent. A small museum relates Sutter's biography and the life of the California pioneers. Our kids were especially taken with the diorama of John Fremont and Kit Carson entering the fort in 1844. The doll that survived the Donner Party disaster is also special. Living History Programs enable groups to actually spend a night at the fort, having spun wool, woven baskets, and prepared their evening meal over fireplaces and in the beehive ovens.

State Indian Museum
2618 K Street, between 26th and 28th streets, Sacramento. (916) 324-0971. Daily 10–5, except holidays. Adults $1; children 6–17, 50¢. Films by request. Groups by appointment. W.

This mesmerizing museum is a treasure house of the Native American world. Dioramas and well-labeled exhibits display Maidus grinding acorns, a Pomo tule boat, headdresses, the ghost dance of the Cheyenne, the healing-child dance, maps, minerals, archaeology, musical instruments, games,

If you've ever wanted to live like a pioneer, the place to do it is Sutter's Fort. Here, the kids make wooden cradles while their parents cook over an open fire.

jewelry, household goods, baskets, and featherwork. Ishi, last of his California tribe, explains his Yahi way of life in photographs, on film, and on tape. Hands-on areas, such as a place to touch different animal pelts and a table to use a mortar and pestle, add spice to the exhibits.

Fairytale Town
William Land Park, 1501 Sutterville Road, I-5 South to Sutterville Road,

Sacramento. (916) 449-5233. February–November, Monday–Friday 10–5, weekends and holidays 10–6 (gate closes ½ hour earlier on weekends and holidays). Closed December and January and when it rains. Children 3–12, 75¢; ages 13–64, $1.50; over 65, $1. Combination tickets to Fairytale Town and the Sacramento Zoo are available at either gate.

Nursery rhymes and favorite stories come to life as children crawl through the Holes in the Cheese, skip along the Crooked Mile, sit in Cinderella's Pumpkin Coach, and slide down the circular slide after visiting Owl's House. You can visit the Three Little Pigs, Mary's Little Lamb, and the Tortoise and the Hare in Farmer Brown's Barn.

Children's birthday parties are held in King Arthur's Castle and in Sherwood Forest daily except Sunday. Special events held monthly. Puppet shows hourly on weekends and school holidays.

Sacramento Zoo

3830 West Land Park Drive, William Land Park, Sacramento. (916) 449-5166. Daily 9–4. Adults $2.50; ages 3–12 and over 65, $1. W.

Over 700 animals live in this tree-shaded garden and zoo. The reptile house is a favorite; others are the wallaroos, the flamingos, and the island of monkeys. New orangutan, tiger, lion, and chimpanzee exhibits show these beautiful animals in natural settings.

Blue Diamond Growers

17th and C streets, Sacramento. (916) 446-8409. Monday–Friday 9, 10, 1, and 2. Saturday, movie only at 11 and 3. Free. Groups by appointment. Tasting room open 9–5:30 weekdays, 10–4 Saturday.

Franciscan fathers brought the almond from Spain to California in 1769. Today Blue Diamond is the world's largest almond packer. Visitors see the many unusual machines designed to sort, crack, halve, slice, dice, and roast almonds. You see concrete silo bins eight stories high, a mile-long conveyor belt, and an explanatory movie on the hour-long tour, then dig into the 12 different flavored almonds in the tasting room.

Sacramento Science Center and Junior Museum
3615 Auburn Boulevard, East Area, Sacramento. (916) 449-8255. Monday–Friday 9:30–5, Sunday 12–5. Adults $2, children $1.

Live animals indigenous to California live in the museum, which also offers special films, exhibits, live animal shows, and a planetarium.

Silver Wings Museum
Mather Air Force Base, Building 3860, Rancho Cordova. Highway 50 east. (916) 364-2177. Monday–Friday 10–4, weekends 12–4. Free. W.

Military and civilian aircraft displays and films dating from the Wright Brothers to Vietnam are presented in this reproduction of a 1914 hangar. There are World War I and World War II aviation displays, models, engines, and a remembrance of pioneer women. The Teeny-Genie, an experimental pleasure plane with a VW engine, is super.

The Mather Planetarium in Rancho Cordova is open to groups by appointment. You'll see stars, planets, comets, meteor showers, outlines of constellations, and other space phenomena on a domed ceiling (916-364-2908).

Nimbus Fish Hatchery
2001 Nimbus Road, Rancho Cordova, on the American River. (916) 355-0666. Daily 8–4. Free. W.

After fighting their way from the Pacific Ocean, salmon and steelhead spawn here each fall and winter. The hatchery has a capacity of twenty million salmon eggs and accounts for 60 to 70 percent of the commercial catch off the California coast. Visitors can see raceway ponds, the fish weir and ladder entrance, a holding pond, the sorting and spawning area, nursery ponds, and the hatchery building.

Gibson Ranch County Park
8552 Gibson Ranch Road, Elverta (take Watt Avenue north to Elverta Road, then turn left on Elverta). (916) 991-9500/991-2066. Daily 8 to dusk; $3 per car. Tours by reservation. All Monday and Tuesday 9–4. Picnic areas.

This 326-acre park is really a working farm. There are cows, hens, and horses to feed; muskrats, ducks, and geese swim in the lake, which you can fish or swim in. There are ponies and horses to ride, paddleboats to rent, old buggies and a blacksmith shop to play with, and hayrides to enjoy.

Folsom Project Dam and Power Plant

7794 Folsom Dam Road, Folsom. (916) 988-1717. Tuesday–Saturday 10 and 1. Free.

Drive on top of the dam and past the gorgeous lake to get to the power-house. Tours pass three generators, with capacities of 66,240 kilowatts each, and go through the dam, depending upon how many people are visiting at the time.

Folsom City Park and Zoo

50 Natoma Street, Folsom. (916) 355-7200. Daily 10–4, except Monday. Free.

This small zoo specializes in California native animals, with some exotic imports. Many of the animals were raised as pets; some are handicapped. None can live wild. The free-roaming flock of peafowl delights visitors. A one-third-scale steam train runs weekends in summer and fall.

Historic Sutter Street, in Folsom, is a restored section of old buildings and shops that reminds visitors of earlier times. At Sutter and Wool streets, the reconstructed Southern Pacific Depot displays historical treasures.

The Folsom Powerhouse, on Riley Street, relayed electricity to Sacramento from 1895 to 1952. For tours call (916) 988-0205.

Western Railway Museum

Rio Vista Junction ten miles east of Fairfield on Highway 12, (707) 374-2978. Weekends and holidays 11–5. Adults $3, juniors and seniors $2, youngsters, $1.

The Western Railway Museum was put together by a nonprofit organization of men who love trains. You can walk through and around the more than 100 retired trolleys and steam locomotives or just watch the railroad buffs at work. An old-fashioned Salt Lake & Utah observation car is a favorite for dreaming (remember Judy Garland in *The Harvey Girls?*), as are the Birney

*Historic Key System streetcar No. 352
ran in Oakland until 1947. Now it's back
in service at The Western Railway
Museum at Rio Vista Junction.*

"dinkey" streetcars, a New York City "el," a Pullman car that's been made
up for sleep, a Toonerville trolley from the Key System, Oakland and San
Francisco streetcars, and many more. The gift shop at the entrance holds
the largest collection of railroad books in the west, along with cards, old
ads, tickets, and badges. Picnic areas are available. Rides are frequent on
weekends.

Rio Vista Museum

*16 North Front Street, Rio Vista. (707) 374-5169. Weekends 2–5, and by
appointment. Free.*

All of the treasures in this little museum have been donated by local residents. There are antique etchings and photos; newspapers and books; and
farm implements such as tools, plows, a buggy, a wagon, a forge, and a
foundry, typewriters, a winepress, Chinese hats, and local birds' eggs. The

museum was created during the Bicentennial, "so," says its curator, "we won't forget all about the past."

Micke Grove Park and Zoo and San Joaquin County Historical Museum

11793 North Micke Grove Road, 3 miles south of Lodi on Highway 99 and on Highway 5. Park: (209) 953-8800. Open dawn to dusk daily; $2.50 per car on weekends and holidays. Rental facility reservations (209) 953-8800/ 331-7400. Zoo: (209) 331-7270; daily 10–5; adults $1.50, children and seniors 50¢. Museum (209) 368-9154; Wednesday–Sunday 1–5; free. Japanese Garden: 9–2; free. W.

This bustling community park offers picnic and play areas, the full range of water sports, a rose garden and a Japanese garden, horseback riding, nature trails, and party facilities. The museum, zoo, and amusement park are all near the main north entrance parking lot.

The seals love applause at the Micke Grove Zoo.

"Man and Nature Hand in Hand" is the theme for the remarkable multi-building museum. In the main building, changing exhibits are always backed up by memories of the pioneer people, including a millinery shop and a Victorian sitting room, both meticulously furnished. On the grounds, you can visit a Tree and Vine building, a Delta building, an 1800s Calaveras schoolhouse, a harness shop, a ranch blacksmith shop, a farm tools and tractor collection, a model of a dairy, and a Sunshine Trail Garden for the Blind. "Earth is so kind, that just tickle her with a hoe and she laughs up a harvest," is what one Delta farmer wrote, while another prophesied, "We will dig gold with a plow."

Lions, bobcats, gray foxes, kinkajous, pumas, and black leopards are some of the animals in this little zoo, now being refurbished. There are daily public feedings of the animals. The seal pool and the tropical forest canopy always draw crowds.

Pixie Woods

Louis Park, Stockton. (209) 466-9890/944-8220. Fall and spring weekends 12–5, Wednesday–Friday 11–5, until 6 on weekends in summer. Closed from Halloween to Easter Week. Over 12, $1, under, 75¢. Train, boat, and merry-go-round, 50¢. Parties by appointment. W.

Stockton's fairyland is for the "young in age and young in heart." You enter through the Rainbow Gates into a magical forest with enchanted lagoons and begin a journey that will take you through some of your favorite fairy-tale settings. Ride the Pixie Express or take a trip on the *Pixie Queen,* a replica of the paddle-wheel steamers that long ago graced the Delta waterways. And be sure to visit Pirates' Cove and the magical volcano. See a puppet show in the Toadstool Theater. Have an adventure in Frontier Town and pet the animals in McDonald's Farm.

The Haggin Museum

1201 North Pershing Avenue, Victory Park, Stockton. Off Highway I-5. (209) 462-4116. Daily 1:30–5, except Monday and holidays. Free. Groups by appointment. W.

Three floors of history and art fill this handsome brick building. Interpretive displays of California and local history include an arcade of 19th-century storefronts, firearms, a firefighters' gallery, and an American Indian gallery. The Holt Hall of Agriculture includes a fully restored 1919 Holt 75 caterpillar tractor and a 1904 combine harvester. The art galleries include work by American artists such as Albert Bierstadt. The letter from Daniel Boone, the Donner Party relics, the port diorama, and the display of 100-year-old dolls are of special interest to kids.

Miller Horse and Buggy Ranch
9425 Yosemite Boulevard, 10 miles east on Highway 132, Modesto. (209) 522-1781. Open "whenever Mrs. Mae Miller is there, which is most of the time." Reservations preferred. Adults $3; children under 12, 50¢ (one adult for every 6 children, please).

This wagon collection and 1900 general store are fascinating, but they are so cluttered that some people may shy away. Those who climb in and poke around will be well rewarded. Over 50 cars and wagons, including stage-coaches, fire engines, beer wagons, racing sulkies, Victoria coaches, excursion buses, and an ambulance used in the San Francisco Earthquake are in the barn. A hurdy-gurdy and high-buttoned shoes, sausage stuffers, old typewriters, and a bicycle collection dating to the 1820s (including a mother-of-pearl tandem bike reputedly given to Lillian Russell by "Diamond Jim" Brady) are in the store.

McHenry Museum
1401 I Street, Modesto. (209) 577-5366. Tuesday–Sunday 12–4. Free. Tours by appointment. W.

"Not to know what happened before one was born is to remain a child," quoth Cicero. And this is the credo of this historical museum, which aims to appreciate the past and the people who pioneered this area. A complete doctor's office, a general store, a re-created blacksmith shop, gold mining paraphernalia, fire-fighting equipment, and a collection of guns and cattle brands are permanent exhibits. Changing displays focus on families, ethnic and religious groups, quilts, fans, dolls, and other areas of interest. Slide shows, movies, and musical events are held in the auditorium.

Down the block, history buffs will want to visit the **McHenry Mansion**, which was built in 1883 and is one of the few surviving reminders of Modesto's past. Today the Italianate mansion has been completely restored and refurbished, right down to the William Morris–designed wallpaper, the rose-brass gas chandelier in the front parlor, the 19th-century English wall-to-wall carpeting, and the newly milled redwood columns on the front veranda. (906 15th Street at I, Modesto; 209-577-5341; group and individual tours by request; free; party rentals).

Hershey Chocolate U.S.A.
1400 South Yosemite Avenue, Oakdale. (209) 847-0381. Monday–Friday 8:15–3, and by appointment. Free.

Candy bars, chocolate kisses, and chocolate syrups are made, weighed, packaged, and labeled in the course of this 30-minute tour. You pass huge chocolate vats, candy-bar molds in action, and rooms for the processing of instant cocoa and chocolate syrup. Samples for chocoholics.

The Gold Country

To drive along Highway 49 is to relive California's history and legends. This is the Gold Country: the land of writers like Mark Twain, Bret Harte, and Joaquin Miller, bandits like Black Bart and Joaquin Murietta, and heros like Ulysses S. Grant and Horatio Alger.

Passing through little towns named Copperopolis and Jenny Lind, visitors who look carefully will see the traces of the hundreds of thousands of people—Cornish, Welsh, English, German, French, Italian, Mexican, Peruvian, Australian, Chinese, and African—who migrated to this place seeking fame and fortune in the "tears from the sun." The town of Volcano still has an old Chinese store and a Jewish cemetery. In Gold Country, you'll find the only town in the United States ever to name itself a nation: Rough and Ready seceded from the Union in April 1850 to become a republic with its own president, constitution, and flag. By July 4, it had slipped quietly back into the United States.

The many parks and campgrounds are usually near quiet streams that once teemed with gold panners. Although there are mining, river-rafting, ballooning, and kayaking expeditions available, to me, the best thing to do in the Gold Country is just explore and talk to the natives. You'll have memorable experiences you couldn't possibly find listed in a book, and you'll hear about towns that exist now only in history books. On the other hand, you could pick up a pan and start sifting. . .

Railtown 1897/The Sierra Railway Company of California State Historic Park
Off Highways 49 and 108 on Fifth Avenue, Jamestown. (209) 984-3593. 10–5 daily in summer, and on fall and spring weekends. Adults $2, seniors and youngsters $1.25. W. Varying times and prices for special train rides. For information: Sierra Railway, P.O. Box 1250, Jamestown, CA 95327.

The Sierra Railway has been working since 1897, and starring in movies since the Marx Brothers went west. After a short film, you'll be guided through the roundhouse to see rolling stock that's starred in over 200 films and TV shows, from *High Noon*, "Petticoat Junction," and "Wild Wild West," to *Mother Lode Cannonball* and *Butch Cassidy and the Sundance Kid*.

Gold Prospecting Expeditions
Old Livery Stable, 18172 Main Street, P.O. Box 974, Jamestown CA, 95327. (209) 984-GOLD. Call for details.

Every day, a tape showing Jamestown's history and how to prospect for gold—and the couple who walked into Ralph Shock's store in January 1985 carrying 11 pounds of gold nuggets in a shopping bag, totalling $140,000—is shown free. There's a "slough" right on the main street of Jamestown for an instant panning experience. Families can go on expeditions that take from an hour to two days, by foot, river raft, or helicopter.

Tuolumne County Museum and History Center
158 West Bradford, Sonora. (209) 532-1317. Monday, Wednesday, Friday 9–4:30; Tuesday, Thursday, Saturday and summer Sundays 10–3:30

This thriving museum salutes Mark Twain with memorabilia, vignettes of the 1890s, and exhibits that tell the exciting story of Tuolumne County. Part of the museum is in the 1857 town jail, and you'll find an old bunkhouse in one jail cell and an extensive gun collection in another, with fascinating tales of the stalwart, independent men who used them. Bill West's cowboy paintings are popular with kids.

Sonora Fire Department Museum
94 North Washington Street, City Hall, Sonora. (209) 532-7432. Daily 10–4. Free.

There's gold on the streets in Jamestown—and you can pan for it if you're a believer.

Speaking trumpets from the 1850s, handmade uniforms from the 1870s, and leather firemen's helmets are displayed along with trophies and hand-operated fire-fighting equipment, including the Eureka No. 1, which was shipped around the Horn from New York in 1876.

Sonora, once called "The Queen of the Southern Mines," is a well-pre-served town. Visitors may be interested in stopping by at the Archaeology and History Display in the A. N. Francisco Building (48 West Yaney Street; free) to see bottles, fragments, and objects found on the site of the building during construction. Another display case contains memorabilia from the 1854 *Union Democrat,* including old type, photos, headlines, and old editions.

Columbia State Historic Park

Highway 49, North of Sonora. (209) 532-4301. Daily 9–5, except Christmas and Thanksgiving. W. Free.

Columbia, "The Gem of the Southern Mines," is the best of the restored gold-mining towns. The streets and wooden sidewalks lead you to buildings, stores, and eateries outfitted as they were in the town's heyday.

The Columbia Gazette office, open to the public on weekends and all summer, still prints a small newspaper; the **Columbia Candy Kitchen** still sells hand-dipped candy; the 1857 **Douglas Saloon** still dispenses an occasional draft beer along with sarsaparilla.

Peek into the carpenter's shop, the ice depot, and the schoolhouse, which has a belltower, a pump organ, a desk, and a potbellied stove. The Chinese herb shop, the fandango hall, the town jail, firehouse, blacksmith shop, and drugstore are other main-street attractions. Fallon House, a Victorian-era hotel, houses a repertory theater and an ice cream parlor. The gold scales in the Wells Fargo Office weighed out over $55 million worth of dust and nuggets of the $87 million mined here. You can also ride a stagecoach and pan for gold!

During **The Hidden Treasure Gold Mine Tour** (532-9693), visitors see the quartz vein that gold formed in millions of years ago, and discover what "side drifts" and "glory holes" are all about (adults $5, children $2.50).

The park museum offers slide shows and exhibits of the Indians, the Chinese population (once one-sixth of Columbia), and the gold miners. Your family could happily spend a day—or a weekend—in this thriving town of yesteryear.

Moaning Cave

Vallecito, on Parrots Ferry Road between Columbia and Highway 4 (209) 736-2708. Forty-five-minute tours 10–4 winter weekdays; 9–6 daily in summer and weekends; closed Christmas. Adults $4.50; children 6–11, $2.25; children under 5 free.

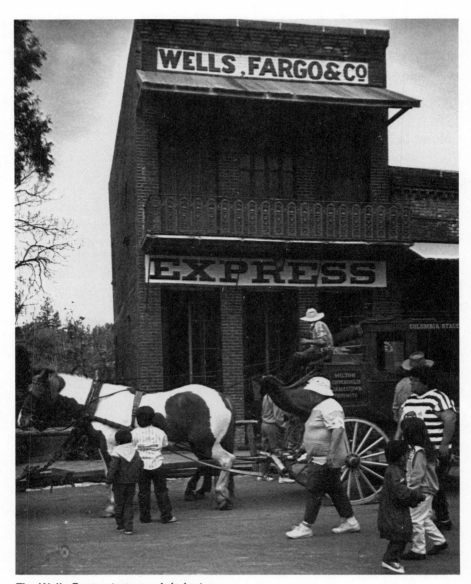

The Wells Fargo stagecoach is just one of the authentic vehicles at Columbia State Historic Park.

You can count the 144 winding steps that lead you 165 feet down a cave with prehistoric bones and moaning sounds. You'll see fantastic rock formations, such as Elephant's Ears and the Little Girl's Face, that add to the eerie feeling that you're intruding on unknown spirits. The main chamber is tall enough to hold the Statue of Liberty. Stalactites hang "tight" from the ceiling, and stalagmites are "mighty mounds" in the floor—that's how we remember which is which. Moaning Cave also offers a three-hour Adventure Tour, with an 180-foot rappel, or rope descent, for ages 12 and up. Picnic tables with a view of the hills offer a pleasant spot to wait, as does the exhibit filled waiting room.

California Caverns
Cave City, Mountain Ranch Road, 9 miles east of San Andreas. (209) 736-2708. P.O. Box 78, Vallecito, CA 95251. 10–5 in summer, 10–4 in fall, weekends in November. Hours depend on the water level inside the cavern. Adults $5, children 6–12, $2.50 for 80-minute "Trail of Light" tour.

"When we emerged into the bright landscapes of the sun everything looked brighter, and we felt our faith in Nature's beauty strengthened, and saw more clearly that beauty is universal and immortal, above, beneath, on land and sea, mountain and plains in heat and cold, light and darkness." John Muir wrote this after wandering through this 200-foot-deep crystalline jungle. California Caverns also offers Wild Cave expedition tours for the adventurous.

Old Timers Museum
470 Main Street, Murphys. (209) 728-3679. Thursday and Friday 9:30–3, Saturday until 4, Sunday 11–4. W. Free.

An old-time bedroom, a bar, a blacksmith shop, a gun collection, photographs, Indian artifacts, and an antique bicycle are the high points of this old-fashioned collection of Gold Country memories.

Tours by appointment also include the historic Murphys Hotel across the street, where the rooms are decorated as they were when people like Ulysses S. Grant, Black Bart, and Mark Twain were guests. Down the block, the Peppermint Stick (209-728-3570) beckons with ice cream specials and peppermint cones.

Mercer Caverns

Ebbetts Pass Highway, 1 mile from Murphys. (209) 728-2101. Daily 9–5 in summer, 11–4 winter weekends and holidays. Adults $4.50; ages 5–11, $2.25.

A 45-minute tour past stalactites and stalagmites, aragonites and helictites, takes you into a subterranean wonderland. Eerie rock formations like the Organ Loft, Angel Wings, and the Chinese Meat Market are dazzling examples of the artistry of nature. Mercer Caverns was discovered in 1885 by a tired, thirsty prospector, Walter J. Mercer, who noticed bay bushes growing near a limestone bluff and thought he had found a well.

Angels Camp Museum

753 Main Street, Angels Camp. (209) 736-4444. 9–5 weekdays, 10–3 weekends. 50¢.

The Gothic Chamber along the Faultwall is a favorite during Centennial Candlelite tours at Mercer Caverns.

A sulkey, a phaeton, a surrey, a hearse, steam tractors, and a mail stage are part of this extensive collection of old wagons and rolling stock. The old mining equipment and the working stamp mill are especially fascinating. Indian artifacts and memorabilia of the country's past are nicely presented. Homage is paid to Mark Twain and the annual Jumping Frog Contest.

Calaveras County Historical Museum
30 Main Street, San Andreas. (209) 754-6513, Daily 10–4. Adults 50¢, children 25¢. W.

The Hall of Records Building in the County Courthouse and Jail has been transformed into a beautifully designed treasure house. You can walk through the judge's chambers (where his robe still hangs) and then go downstairs to see the cell where Black Bart awaited trial. The museum focuses on the Miwok way of life and on the people living in San Andreas during the 1880s, with representative rooms and exhibits.

Amador County Museum
225 Church Street, Jackson (209) 223-3230, ext. 386. Wednesday–Sunday 10–4. Donation.

Working scale models of Kennedy Mine Tailing Wheel No. 2 and the Kennedy Mine head frame, a gold room tracing the history of the area from the discovery of gold to the advent of hard rock machinery, and a Congress of Curiosities—almost an old-fashioned Sears Roebuck catalog come to life—make this cheerful museum a pleasant stop. The children's bedroom and the chair used by a woman while driving her own covered wagon west are personal favorites.

One mile out of town on North Main Street, there are two wheels on each side of the road, each 58 feet in diameter. They were used to transport waste from the mine to a reservoir a half mile away. Almost lost in history, the huge wheels are still impressive.

Chaw'se Indian Grinding Rock State Historic Park
14881 Pine Grove–Volcano Road, 11 miles north of Jackson. (209) 296-7488. Day use: $3 per car. Cultural center open daily 11–4 in winter, longer in summer.

At first, the huge flat limestone bedrock, 173 feet long and 82 feet wide, doesn't look like it's worth a second glance. But then you look closer and discover the petroglyphs scratched in by the Miwok Indians to commemorate their hunting and fishing tales. The 1,185 "pockmarks" are actually mortar holes where the women ground the seeds, bulbs, funghi, and acorns that served as the staples of their diet. Each of the mortar holes was abandoned when it became too deep. The acorn meal was sifted and washed many times to remove bitterness, then the meal was mixed with water in a basket and heated by hot rocks dropped into the mush. Each family consumed about 2,000 pounds of acorns a year. Visitors may also see a ceremonial roundhouse, a granary, eight bark dwelling houses, and a hand-game house.

Chew Kee Store
Fiddletown, just off Highway 49 outside Plymouth on the way to Volcano. Summer, 12–4, Saturdays 12–4. Free.

Build in the 1850s, the Chew Kee Store is believed to be California's only surviving rammed-earth structure from the Gold Rush era. The small store is a remarkable example of history frozen in time, "a fly in amber," since Jimmy Yee lived there from 1913 to 1965 and didn't change a thing. It's still a Chinese herb store, with ceramic rice crocks, brass opium cans, gambling hall receipts, prayers, and two spare back rooms left just as they were when Dr. Yee, Jimmy's guardian, died. The devoted local history buffs who take care of the store will be glad to tell you about it.

Daffodil Hill
Three miles north of Volcano on Shake Ridge Road from Fiddletown. (209) 223-0608/622-2129. Mid-March to mid-April, 10–5 daily. Free.

Although it's only open when the daffodils are in bloom around Easter, this is worth a stop. The McLaughlins have planted about 300,000 daffodils in many colors, and, between the flowers and the 11 peacocks walking around, they have created an enchanted hillside.

Sam's Town Americana Museum

Cameron Park, Highway 50, Shingle Springs. (916) 933-1662. May–mid-September: Sunday–Thursday 8 a.m.–8:30 p.m., until 9:30 weekends; September–April; Sunday–Thursday 8–8, until 9 weekends. Ages 8 to 69, $1.

If you close your eyes and ignore the sawdust-laden dining rooms, game room, and Gay 90s store and go through the red velvet curtains, you'll discover a fine wax museum with 29 historical vignettes including Lillie Coit and her horse-drawn fire engine, Abraham and Mary Todd Lincoln, a millinery shop, a barber-shop-with-quartet, Jenny Lind, Lillian Russell, and Huckleberry Finn.

Vintage vehicles and movie memorabilia, such as Charlton Heston's cage from *Planet of the Apes,* stand on the grounds, which has a super "old-town" facade.

El Dorado County Historical Museum

100 Placerville Drive, El Dorado County Fairgrounds. (916) 626-2250. Wednesday–Saturday 10–4. W. Free.

"Smokers and chewers will please spit on each other and not on the stove or the floor." This sign is one of many in this big old barn of a museum staffed by caring volunteers. There's an old cash register run by steel balls, lots of dolls, a Civil War viewing casket, two well-stocked country stores, Snow Shoe Thompson's nine-foot skis, a surrey with a fringe on top, and lots more. Right outside the door, a mammoth shaking table, for separating gold from ore, and a walk-in Shay engine No. 4 grabs kids' attention.

In town, check out the **Fountain and Tallman Soda Factory Museum,** at 524 Main Street (626-0773).

Gold Bug Mine

Bedford Park, a mile north of downtown at the end of Bedford Avenue, Placerville. (916) 622-0832. Open daily. Free.

The only municipally owned, open-to-the-public gold mine in the world was worked as recently as 1947. The longer shaft of the mine ends at an exposed gold-bearing quartz vein. The occasional drip of water rings in the cool, eerie silence of the tunnel. The huge gold-stamp mill by the creek is run by park rangers on weekends.

Placerville was originally called Old Hangtown, after the hanging tree in

Penny candies, buttons and knickknacks
are for sale at this Gold Rush store in the
El Dorado County Historical Museum.

This antique trick mirror is just one of the treasures in the memory filled El Dorado County Historical Museum.

the center of town. The Pony Express and Wells Fargo offices are still there to see. In one week during the Gold Rush, two Englishmen found $17,000 worth of gold in the main street of town. It is said that the legendary Hangtown Fry originated here when a miner walked into a restaurant and demanded a meal that used the three most expensive ingredients at once: eggs, bacon, and oysters.

Marshall Gold Discovery State Historic Park
Highway 49, Coloma (916) 622-3470. Museum: Daily 10–5 except holidays, 11–5 in winter. W. Adults $1. Park: 8–sunset. Picnicking: $3 per car.

"This day some kind of mettle found in the tailrace . . . looks like goald." A millworker noted this in his diary in January 1848. The gold found changed the face of California—and America.

Sutter's Mill has risen again on the American River. Across the highway, a modern museum is dedicated to the discovery of gold and the lives of the gold miners. Maps, tools, mementos, and pictures are displayed against informational panels and dioramas. Films narrated by Hugh "Wyatt Earp" O'Brien bring history to life. On the grounds, follow a self-guiding trail to see the mill; a Chinese store; a mine; a miner's cabin furnished with corn, beans, a scale, a Bible, and the miner in bed; a Mormon's cabin; an arrastre (ore crusher); and a town that's almost disappeared. If you feel lucky, bring your own gold pan and boots.

Placer County Historical Museum
Gold County Fairgrounds, 1273 High Street, Auburn. (916) 855-9570. Tuesday–Sunday 10–4. Adults $1, ages 6–16 and over 65, 50¢.

Old mining equipment and pioneer mementos recall the early days of Placer County. Artifacts from Auburn's former Chinese community, the assayer's office, Indian relics, and walk-through model mine are informative. The exhibits change regularly.

Also on the grounds, at 291 Auburn-Folsom Road, is the **Bernhard Museum Complex**. Benjamin Bernhard's home and winery and cooperage are open, with tours by volunteer docents. The admission ticket serves for both places.

Placer County has recently opened two new historical museums: **The Griffith Quarry Museum** and the **Forest Hill Museum**. Griffith Quarry, in Griffith Park, is open from 12 to 4 on weekends and displays material on the granite works, the Griffith family, and the area. Forest Hill Museum is in Memorial Park in Forest Hill.

North Star Mine Powerhouse Museum

Lower Mill Street, at Empire, Grass Valley. (916) 273-9853. Daily 11–5 in summer. Adults $1.

Built by A.D. Foote in 1875, this is the first completely water-powered compressed-air transmission plant of its kind. The compressed air, generated by ten-ton, 30-foot Pelton waterwheels, furnished power for the mine. The museum houses photos, ore specimens, safes, dioramas and models of the mines, an assaying laboratory, and a working Cornish pump. The star of the show is the 30-foot Pelton Wheel itself.

Grass Valley Museum

Mount St. Mary's, South Church and Chapel streets. (916) 272-5154. Wednesday, Saturday, and Sunday in summer, 12–3. Free.

A schoolroom, an 1880s doctor's office, children's bedrooms, a lace collection, and a glass slipper collection mix with convent memories in this quaint museum.

Empire Mine State Historic Park

10791 East Empire Street, Grass Valley. (916) 273-8522. 10–5 daily except holidays. Adults $1. Group tours. W.

Grass Valley is another nicely preserved Gold Rush town. While browsing, you may want to see the homes of Lola Montez and Lotta Crabtree on Mill Street. Lola was a Bavarian singer, dancer, and king's favorite who fled to America in 1853 when her king fell from power. Lotta Crabtree was Lola's protégée and soon became famous, rich, and beloved by the American public. Lola's home is open to the public daily, 12 to 4; free in summer.

Keeping alive the story of hard-rock gold mining and its significance in California's history, the Empire is the oldest, largest, and richest gold mine in the area. Many of the 16 stopping points along the mine's self-guided tour are in ruins, and the sites are being reconstructed. And the William Bourn family "cottage" is furnished and open for tours. Movies, films, and living history days will help excite your imagination so you'll think of the

***Little miners practice with this drill at
the Empire Mine.***

hundreds of Cornish miners who dug the 367 miles of tunnels, almost
11,000 feet deep, and the mules that pulled the ore trains through the tunnels. Enterprising souls will want to know that there's still gold in there.

   To relive a bit of history, have a Cornish pasty at one of the bakeries in
town. The miners called these meat and potato pies "letters from home."

Nevada County Historical Society Museum

Firehouse No. 1, Main and Commercial streets, Nevada City. (916) 265-9941. Daily 11–4 in summer, Tuesday–Sunday in winter. Donation.

Located in one of the quaint town's most photogenic buildings, the museum has just been completely refurbished. Maidu Indian artifacts, relics of the Donner Party, children's toys and books, a Chinese altar, showshoes for horses, the photograph of a miner with the image of himself as a 12-year-old appearing mysteriously on the film, and pioneer memories will fill the space.

Nevada City, the best of the gold-mining towns, is a thriving community with the feel of turn-of-the-century Gold Country. Walking along the narrow streets is a pleasure. Visitors may want to stop at the **Searls Historical Library** (214 Church Street; 365-5910; Monday–Saturday 1–4); the very strange conglomeration that calls itself the **American Victorian Museum** (325 Spring Street, 265-5804), which is also a dinner theater; and the **Orey Victorian Tour House** (401 North York Street; 265-9250), a pretty pink Victorian.

Malakoff Diggins State Historic Park

North Bloomfield Star Route, 17 miles northeast of Nevada City on a crooked mountain road. (916) 265-2740. Museum: daily 10–5 in summer, and on weekends in spring and fall. Camping and picnicking, $3 per car. Tours by appointment.

Many millions of dollars' worth of gold poured from these huge hydraulic diggings, and a small sign tells visitors that there's still enough gold left here, and on other sites around the area, to mine $12 million annually for the next 50 years. This park is a silent monument to the hydraulic miners. The museum displays a model of the monitor used in gold mines and shows how hydraulic mining worked. Photos of the two-mile Bloomfield tunnel, 12-foot-long miners' skis, a portable undertaker's table, mementos of the Chinese miners, and an old-time bar and poker room are some of the highlights. Walkers can also see a drugstore, a general store, and a livery filled with wagons. Films round out the experience.

Sierra County Museum

Main Street, Downieville. Daily 10–5 in summer, weekends in spring and fall, and by appointment. 50¢.

Keepsakes of the hardy pioneers of Downieville are housed in this old stone building. Outside is a scale model of an arrastre from the Sierra Buttes Mine that crushed ore more finely than the tailings from a stamp mill, along with a hand-operated 100-year-old valve used to control water pressure in the early hydraulic diggings at Morristown.

Kentucky Mine Museum and Sierra County Historical Park
Highway 49, 1 mile north of Sierra City. (916) 862-1310. Daily 10–5, Memorial Day–September 30; weekends in October. Gold mine and stamp mill tour $1, museum 50¢.

A five-stamp mill built in the 1879s, a 1928 ten-stamp mill, and a hard-rock gold mine are shown during a fine 40-minute tour that explains the process of hard-rock mining from beginning to end. The stamp mill is one of the only mills in the area that is still operable, with all the original machinery intact. The Pelton waterwheels still work, too. The museum shows constantly changing displays from Sierra County's past, including mining equipment, logging machinery, clothing, skis, household articles, and a schoolroom exhibit. There are outdoor concerts in summer.

Plumas-Eureka State Park Museum
310 Johnsville Road, off county road 89, Blairsden. (916) 836-2380. Museum: daily 9–5 in summer and fall, weekends in winter. W. Free.

Snowshoe Thompson used to carry 60 to 80 pounds of mail on his back over the Sierra in winter for the miners. A pair of his extra-long skis are displayed in this packed museum, along with hard-rock mining displays, an assay office, models of a stamp mill, an arrastre, natural history exhibits, and pioneer life remembrances. The outbuildings are fun, too.

Sierra Valley Museum
Loyalton City park, Loyalton. (916) 993-4454. Wednesday–Sunday 12–4, Memorial Day–October. Free.

A small but warm volunteer-run museum of 19th-century Sierra Valley remembers the pioneers, housewives, miners, and businessmen who tamed the Sierra Valley.

Plumas County Museum
500 Jackson, Quincy. (916) 283-1750. Monday–Friday and weekends in summer, 8–5. W. Free.

This living museum depicts local history and artifacts, lumbering and mining displays, and an outstanding collection of Maidu Indian baskets.

Donner Memorial State Park
Donner Lake, Truckee. (916) 587-3841. Daily 10–12 and 1–4. Adults $1; children 6–17, 50¢.

During the disastrous winter of 1846, a party of 89 tried to make it through the mountains to California. Only 47 people survived, and it's believed that some survivors resorted to cannibalism. The Emigrant Trail Museum combines natural history with accounts of the conquest of the Sierra Nevada. The tragic story of the Donner Party is told with relics, dioramas, pictures, and models. The pedestal of the memorial to the Donner Party is 22 feet high—as high as the early snowfall that trapped them. Chinese railroad workers, the "Big Four" railroad tycoons, miners, and mountain men are also remembered here.

Lake Tahoe
Lake Tahoe Visitors Authority, P. O. Box 16299, South Lake Tahoe, CA 95706; (916) 544-5050. North Tahoe Visitors and Convention Bureau, P. O. Box 5578, Tahoe City, CA 95730; (916) 583-3494. Road conditions: (800) 822-5977.

Lake Tahoe is justifiably world-famous for its crystal-clear water and beautiful setting. Visitors can ski, water-ski, boat, swim (only in August unless you're a polar bear), sun, golf, windsail, hike, and enjoy the forest wilderness and the exhilarating clarity of the air and sunshine.

Naturalist programs are given on summer weekends in the D.L. Bliss and Emerald Bay state parks and at Camp Richardson. The **Taylor Creek Stream Profile Chamber** near Camp Richardson is part of the El Dorado National Forest Visitors Center. You can take one of the self-guided nature walks through a mountain meadow and marsh and down into chamber for a fish-eye view of a mountain stream. Recorded messages help identify the fish and plants in front of you.

Vikingsholm Castle, a 38-room Nordic fortress, is open to the public 10–5 daily, in summer, on Emerald Bay's southwest shore.

The **Tahoe Queen's Glass Bottom Boat** is a Mississippi paddle wheeler that shows you another view of the lake. Other boats cruise the blue waters as well. (916) 541-3364. Sails at 11 a.m., 1:30 and 3:55 p.m. June–September; noon daily in winter. Adults $13; children 11 and under $6 (also dinner cruises).

The **Lake Tahoe Historical Society Log Cabin Museum** on Star Lake Avenue (10–4 daily in summer) features artifacts from Tahoe's early days. The **Western American Ski Sports Museum** features ski exhibits from 1860 to the present, vintage ski movies, and artifacts of Snowshoe Thompson (Boreal Ridge exit, I-80; 916-426-3313; Tuesday–Friday 12–4, Saturday–Sunday 11–5; free).

Venture to the Nevada side of the lake for a visit to the **Ponderosa Ranch** (Incline Village; 702-831-0691; 10–5 daily in summer, weekends in spring and fall) to see the Cartwright Ranch House, Hoss's Mystery Mine, Frontier Town, an antique car and carriage museum, the Ponderosa barnyard, and other attractions.

But you'll always head back to the glorious lake, gouged from the crown of the Sierra during the ice ages and named, in the language of the Washoe tribe, "Big Water."

The Fresno Area and Madera County

Some people think that Fresno exists only as a stopping-off place from San Francisco to Los Angeles, although it's a big, booming city. The trip to Fresno is four hours by car from San Francisco, but there are so many motels you can usually be assured of a room when you arrive. Surrounded by orchards and rich farmland, pretty lakes, and an impressive irrigation system, Fresno is also the gateway to Sierra National Forest, and Sequoia, Kings Canyon, and Yosemite national parks. Hiking, skiing, spelunking, and wandering through groves of the largest living things on earth—the giant sequoia redwoods—are all 40 minutes away. Closer to Fresno, seven lakes offer sailing, fishing, houseboating, waterskiing, and windsurfing.

R. C. Baker Memorial Museum
297 West Elm, Coalinga. (209) 935-1914. Monday–Friday 9–12 and 1–5, Saturday 11–5, Sunday 1–5. Free.

The remodeled R. C. Baker Museum, named in honor of a Coalinga pioneer, oilman, and inventor, shows both the natural and manmade history of Coalinga. The land surrounding Coalinga is rich with oil and minerals, and the museum emphasizes these assets. Oil is also responsible for the numerous well-preserved fossils found near here, including mastodon skeletons and an oil-preserved primeval lizard. Artifacts of the first people to live here, the Tachi tribe of the Yokut nation, include evidence that they used oil for trading. The crowded 1910 kitchen, 1880 advertising cards, a collection of porcelain and glass insulators for telephone poles, and the doll collection are among the museum's highlights. Two of the most unusual treasures are 600 kinds of barbed wire, dating from 1867, and a 1908 quilt made of the silk swatches that were packed in Nebo cigarettes. There's even a surrey "with the fringe on top." The back room holds tools and machinery used in the oil fields.

Visitors to Coalinga will enjoy a drive nine miles north on Highways 33 and 198 past the Grasshopper oil pumps: oil field characters painted in many colors to look like clowns, birds, and animals.

Tulare County Museum
63 South Mooney Boulevard, Mooney Grove Park, Visalia. (209) 733-6616.
Thursday–Monday in winter, Wednesday–Monday in summer. 50¢.

"End of the Trail," the bronze sculpture by James Earl Fraser portraying a tired Indian on a pony—once the most copied piece of art in the world—is the star attraction at this lively museum. That sculpture was first exhibited in San Francisco in 1915 at the Panama-Pacific Exposition. A one-room schoolhouse, newspaper and dental offices, and rooms from turn-of-the-century homes re-create the past. Furniture, clothes, cooking utensils, toys, baskets, World War I uniforms, and early farm machinery are on exhibit.

The 143-acre park offers picnic arbors and oak trees, boating, skateboard tracks, and more.

The Depot Restaurant
207 East Oak Street at Church, Railway Square, Visalia. (209) 732-8611.
Monday–Saturday 11–10. W.

"All aboard that's going aboard" is a famous cry that rang out in the Depot building over 80 years ago, when the waiting room was filled with people taking trains to different parts of the country. Now diners can enjoy the richly decorated train station while they dine on steak, chicken, and lobster.

Tulare Historical Museum
444 West Tulare Avenue, Tulare. (209) 686-2074. Thursday–Saturday 10–4, Sunday 12:30–4. Donation. W.

"Take a trip back in time" is the theme of this historic museum. You're greeted at the door by a life-sized horse and a doctor's buggy, then step back to a Yokuts village around Tulare Lake. Walk through the coming of the railroad, the lives of some of the early settlers, the three great fires that swept Tulare during its first 14 years, and the incorporation of the city. Mini-replicas of rooms in an early Tulare home and local businesses revivify a time gone by.

Boyden Cavern
Kings Canyon National Park, Highway 180, 77 miles east of Fresno. (209) 736-2708. Daily 10–5, June–September; daily 11–4, May and October. Adults $4, children $2, seniors $3.50.

A 45-minute tour takes you into a wondrous world deep beneath the 2,000-foot-high marble walls of the famous Kings Gates. Massive stalagmites, delicate stalactites, and splendid arrays of crystalline formations defy description. Boyden Cavern is in the deepest canyon in the United States.

Clovis Big Creek Historical Museum
401 Pollasky Avenue, Clovis. (209) 297-8033. Thursday and Friday 11–3, Saturday 10–4. Donation.

Artifacts from the first families of Clovis help make the past understandable to the present.

Porterville Historical Museum
257 North D Street. (209) 784-2053. Thursday, Friday, Saturday 10–5; Sunday 12–4; and by appointment. W. Free.

The old Southern Pacific Railroad Station houses an interesting collection of artifacts of Porterville's pioneer men and women. Cameras, guns, saddles, stuffed animals (including a California condor), office equipment, Yokut basketry, and the turn-of-the-century kitchen, dining room, and pharmacy all make history come alive for the young and rekindle memories in the hearts and minds of older citizens.

Zalud House

Southwest corner of Morton and Hockett, Porterville. (209) 784-1400, ext. 461. Wednesday–Saturday 10–4, Sunday 2–4. Adults 50¢, children 25¢. Groups by appointment. Videotape oral histories and films. W.

One of the state's unsung treasures is this remarkably preserved and lovingly cared-for Victorian home. Pearle Zalud was born here in 1884 and lived there until her death in 1981. Her world tour, at age 19, was the first of many, and the home bears the beautiful fruits of her souvenir hunting. The house is exactly as she left it—which is exactly as her father liked it in

The engaging curator at the Zalud House loves telling stories and sharing the wonders of this fly-in-amber historical home.

1912, when her mother died. The art and furnishings, the hats, dolls, collars and laces, the framed antique valentines, and the family photos all create a house that is a home.

Porterville is lucky enough to have been given not only the house and its contents, but also an extremely able and caring curator who has spent years documenting and cleaning all the Zaluds' belongings, including linens and clothing bought half a century ago and never taken out of the original boxes, and pantry supplies including a 1909 can of baking powder and a 1912 gas stove that still works. The curator really enjoys sharing this world with visitors, and children are fascinated by the story of Pearle's brother Edward, a cowboy who was killed while riding, and her brother-in-law William, who was shot to death by a woman in the Porterville Pioneer Hotel in 1917. The chair with the bullet hole is upstairs.

Since there was so much left in the closets, the curator changes the exhibits in the rooms with the seasons. The beautiful flower gardens outside are available for private parties and weddings.

Colonel Allensworth State Historic Park
Twenty miles north of Wasco on Highway 43, 9 miles west of Earlimart on Highway 99, Sotourna Avenue, Allensworth. (805) 849-3433. To schedule a tour, write Star Route 1, P. O. Box 148, Allensworth, CA 93219.

The only California town to be founded, financed, and governed by Black Americans is being restored to its 1908 state. A visitors' center with exhibits and films, a picnic area, two museums, the Colonel's residence, and the original schoolhouse are open to the public on request, as is the 15-unit campground. The Mary Dickinson Memorial Library is open now, as is the Morris Smith House and the Hinsman Family Home, which is open to overnight guests who want to experience living in the past.

Lindsay Olive Growers
Route 65 to West Hermosa to Westwood, Lindsay. (209) 562-3082. Monday–Friday 10–4. Groups by appointment. W. Free.

Did you know that a single large black olive has 4.54 calories in it? And lots of calcium? Visit the Lindsay Olive factory showroom and watch a 20-minute film "tour" about the history of the olive and California, and tips on how to grow, pick, and cure olives while you taste to your heart's content. Tools and olive wood crafts are displayed.

Don's Exotic Animal Farm
14901 South Highland, Selma, CA. (209) 896-0691.

Foxes, monkeys, llamas, bears, anacondas, Belgian horses, and other strange and wonderful creatures may be seen by appointment.

Pioneer Village Museum
Adjoining Highway 99, Art Gonzales Parkway, Selma. (209) 896-8871. Seasonal hours. Adults $2, seniors $1.50, children 50¢, groups $1.25. W.

Victorian homes and cherished buildings are being moved to, and restored in, this museum-in-progress. Visitors walk through a museum store and out on the grounds to a 1904 Victorian Queen Anne, the old bar built by a Civil War veteran, Selma's 1887 Southern Pacific Depot, a 1901 little red schoolhouse, a steepled church, a doctor's office, a barber shop, a pottery shop, a newspaper office, and the Ungar Opera House.

Kearney Mansion and Kearney Park
Kearney Park, 7 miles west of downtown Fresno, 7160 West Kearney Boulevard, Fresno. (209) 441-0862. Friday–Sunday 1–4. Adults $2; ages 13–17, $1; children under 12, 75¢. Groups by appointment.

Built between 1900 and 1903, the restored home of M. Theo Kearney, pioneer Fresno land developer and raisin baron, has preserved many of the original furnishings, including European wallpapers, art nouveau light fixtures, and replicas of original carpets and wallpapers.

Discovery Center
1944 North Winery Avenue, Fresno (Highway 9 to McKinley, then east). (209) 251-5531. Tuesday–Sunday 11–5. Adults $1.50; children 5–16, $1.25. Group rates. Summer astronomy program. Picnic and playgrounds. W.

This hands-on science center helps children try things out for themselves. There's a bubble machine, a tree that lights up by sound, a feel box, a reaction machine, a laser beam, pipe phones, and a peripheral-vision tester. The Indian room has a Yokut hut and shows the many things that the Indian has introduced to civilization. Dioramas of the animal and vegetable life of the valley are also fun to look at. Children have a great time here.

Fresno Arts Center
2233 North First Street, between Clinton and McKinley avenues. (209) 485-4810. Tuesday–Sunday, 10–5. Adults $2, students and seniors $1. Weekends free. W.

A forum for the arts of the 19th and 20th centuries, with revolving exhibits, classes, tours, and lectures.

Also in town: **Meux Home Museum** (1007 R Street at Tulare; 209-233-8007; Friday–Sunday 12–4; $2 adults, 75¢ students; groups by appointment), a sweet blue and white Queen Anne with docents who enjoy talking about Victorian family life and explaining how things worked back when.

Danish Museum (1800 North Maroa Avenue; 266-1335; Wednesday 10–1, and by appointment), a collection of memorabilia concerning genealogy, Danish immigration to the valley, valley history, and a Danish library.

German Museum (3233 North West Avenue; 229-8287; Monday–Friday 12–4, Saturday 9:30–12), run by the American Historical Society of Germans from Russia.

Fresno Metropolitan Museum of Art, History and, Science
1515 Van Ness Avenue, Fresno. (209) 441-1444. Wednesday–Sunday 11–5. Adults $2; seniors and students $1; children 3–12, 75¢. Tours by appointment. W.

A work in progress, this shiny new museum in the old *Fresno Bee* building offers changing exhibits of american art, and regional history and science. Some of the permanent exhibits include William Saroyan's bicycle, Ansel Adams prints, and a doll collection. In a room full of Yosemite stagecoaches and wagons, you can read eyewitness accounts such as this man's trip in 1884; "We tried all possible devices to steady ourselves, and to avoid concussion of the spine, which really appeared inevitable. . . . at last we entered the true forest belt and anything more beautiful you cannot conceive. We forgot our bumps and bruises in sheer delight. Oh the loveliness of the pines and cedars. . . . "

Shirley Temple, Betty Boop, Kewpie, and Little Women, are some of the dolls in the Fresno Museum's collection, dating from 1870 to 1950.

Fresno Zoo, Storyland, and Rotary Playland

894 West Belmont Avenue, Roeding Park, Fresno. Freeway 99 between Olive and Belmont. (209) 264-5988. Zoo: Children over 14, $3; children 4–14, $1. 10–5 daily October–March, until 6:30 April–September. W. Storyland: $1.75 for those over 3, daily 10–5, May–Labor Day; weekends and holidays 10–5 rest of year (closed December–President's weekend in February). Zoo free first Wednesday of month. Strollers and wheelchairs available. Playland: 486-2124. Prices and hours vary depending on season; usually, 10 to dusk, when school's out. Boating costs also vary.

The Fresno Zoo is one of the most progressive in the country. In the South American Tropical Rain Forest Exhibit, visitors walk through a lush habitat of free-flying birds and small primates. The computerized state-of-the-art reptile house has been extremely successful in breeding almost-extinct animals. The elephants thrive in the waterfall and deep pool in their section. Winding paths and lush foliage add to the pleasure of a stroll through the zoo, as does the Ask Me! cart program. Kids especially like meeting hawks and owls face to face when the docent takes them out of their cages for discussions with visitors.

In **Storyland,** talking storybook keys ($1.75) persuade the blue caterpillar to tell eight classic fairytales. Then when children have heard the stories, they can go on to visit the heroes of the tales. They can play in King Arthur's castle, Red Riding Hood's grandmother's cottage, Mr. Toad's cart,

Hawks and great horned owls are just some of the critters taken on walks by docents at the Fresno Zoo.

or they can talk to Simple Simon's pie man, the knaves of Alice's court, or Little Miss Muffet and Winnie the Pooh.

Children will find **Rotary Playland** irresistible. There's a roller coaster, a Ferris wheel, a kiddie car, ride, a scenic miniature train ride, a merry-go-round, concessions, and picnic areas. Paddleboats, motorboats, and rowboats to rent by the hour on Lake Washington also attract the seaworthy.

Fort Millerton, also in the park (441-0862; weekends 1–4 May 1–September 30; donation), houses a small exhibit of pioneer life, with antique toys, lumber tools, and the medical kit of Fresno's first doctor.

San Joaquin Fish Hatchery
Friant, off Highway 41, 13 miles northeast of Fresno. (209) 822-2374. Daily 8–4:30. Free.

There are more fish in this one spot than you'll ever see again: more than two million trout in sizes that range from pinheads to fingerlings ready to catch are raised in these trout-hatching ponds. Four times a day the fish are fed high-protein dry pellets. When they're a year old and ten inches long, they're taken in tanks by plane and truck to the heavily fished lakes and streams of California. But while they're here, it's really fun to walk along the 48 ponds and watch the fish leap over and slide down the little dams between them. A photo exhibit explains about trout habits and the trout-seeding program.

Friant Dam and Millerton Lake State Recreational Area
Off Highway 41, north of Fresno. (209) 822-2212. Open daily daylight hours. $2 per car to enter park.

Fed by Sierra snows, the waters of Millerton Lake are released into the Friant-Kern irrigation canals to feed the rich croplands of Fresno County. The dam is 319 feet high and 3,488 feet long, with a reservoir capacity of 5.2 million gallons. You can walk halfway across the dam while guides tell you the history of the project. The old Millerton Courthouse, overlooking the dam, is a pleasant little museum of Friant history (open by appointment; 209-822-2332).

Madera County Museum
210 West Yosemite, Madera. (209) 673-0291. Off Highway 99 from Fresno. Weekends 1–4, and by appointment. Free.

Three floors of displays emphasize the county's mining, logging, and agricultural history in this 1900 granite courthouse. The displays include an Indian room, a country store, a miner's cabin, a blacksmith shop, and a Victorian bedroom and a parlor room. The section of the flume of the Madera Sugar Pine Lumber Company is overwhelming. The "downtown" room shows what the city looked like in 1900 and even has a stagecoach in which people rode to Yosemite Park.

Sierra Mono Indian Museum
Intersection of Roads 225 and 228, North Fork (off Highway 41 from Fresno on the way to Bass Lake). (209) 877-2115. Monday–Saturday 9–4, and by appointment. Adults $1.50, high schoolers $1, grade schoolers 75¢.

The only Indian museum in California solely owned and operated by an Indian tribe without any outside help, the Sierra Mono Indian Museum is a triumph of care, hard work, and attention to detail. The dioramas of wildlife in nature and vignettes portraying Indian foods and culture are well labeled and beautifully designed. Did you know that rattlesnakes are born alive, not hatched from eggs? You can see some unborn baby rattlesnakes if you look carefully. The museum offers classes and demonstrations on basketmaking, beadwork, acorn gathering, and other arts and crafts.

Old Town
North Fork (Highway 41 from Fresno; turn right at Road 200; take the North Fork turnoff; turn left on 221, then drive 4 miles to North Fork and 2½ miles down Road 226.) (209) 877-2895/642-3185. Weekends and Wednesday–Sunday in summer, 10–5.

A small town of Old Country cabins, a little country church, a jail with a "man" on the bunk and two others playing cards, and a few stores and restaurants. You'll find a hearse on its way to Boot Hill, a caboose, a fire engine and wagons on the streets. The town is very rustic and authentic, and on summer weekends, old-time gunfighters have been known to shoot it out on the streets while a rodeo goes on out back.

Fresno Flats Historic Park
School Road (Road 427, off Highway 41), Oakhurst. (209) 683-6570/7766. Tuesday–Saturday 1–3, Sunday 1–4. Costumed docents will host groups by appointment. Write SHSA, P.O. Box 451, Oakhurst, CA 93644. Free. Picnic area.

Designed to capture the flavor of family life in Central California's foothills and mountains a century ago, Fresno Flats preserves buildings along with memories. The old Fresno Flats school is now a museum with interesting artifacts and revolving exhibits, but the Laramore-Lymon 1867 farmhouse and the 1869 Taylor log house are living museums. A jail, a blacksmith shop, an old barn, a wagon-state collection, and a flume are also on the grounds. One side of the Taylor log house is furnished as a late-19th-century living room, and the other contains the re-creation of an early-day forest ranger's office complete with maps, old tools, and a display of how the house was constructed.

Mariposa County History Center
12th and Jessie, Mariposa, off Highway 49. (209) 966-2924. Daily 10–5, weekends only in winter. Donation.

In what has been called "the finest small museum to be seen anywhere," you'll see a typical one-room miner's cabin with all his worldly possessions; the more comfortable home of the west's most famous explorer, John C. Fremont, and his wife Jessie; a street of shops reminiscent of the 1850s; a one-room schoolhouse; and art and artifacts showing how gold was formed and extracted. Of special interest are the "Dear Charlie" letters posted throughout—letters written by Horace Snow from 1852 through 1854 to Charlie, his boyhood friend in Cambridge, Massachusetts. They give a miner's-eye view of life in the mines more than a century ago. The five-stamp mill, the Indian village with its bark houses and sweat house, and the mining exhibits on the grounds are also worth seeing.

Nearby, at Tenth and Bullion streets, is the *Mariposa County Courthouse* (966-3222; Monday–Friday 9–5 in winter, weekends April–October, and by appointment; free), the oldest courthouse still in use in California. The clock in the tower has been marking time since 1866.

California's State Mining and Mineral Exhibit, now in downtown Mariposa where State Highways 140 and 49 meet (9 to 4 daily; adults $2, seniors $1, under 12 free; groups by appointment) is in the process of moving to a fabulous new site at the Mariposa County Fairgrounds. The 20,000-piece collection will flourish on a hillside where forty-niners once mined the gold-rich ore. Mining equipment, picnic spots, hands-on experience with models, and a 200-foot mine tunnel to walk through are in the works.

Yosemite Mountain Sugar Pine Railroad

Highway 41, Yosemite Mountain, Fish Camp. (209) 683-7273. Adults $5–$7, children $2.75–$3.75. Moonlight specials include a New York steak barbecue with entertainment around the campfire. Call for times and prices.

Just four miles from Yosemite Basin, this scenic, historic narrow-gauge steam railroad and logging train wends its way through four miles of forest, past Slab Town Loop and Honey Hill and down to the bottom of Lewis Creek Canyon. You can stop there and have a picnic, then return on a later train. The Jenny logger steam train operates daily from mid-April to November 1, except when the steam logger runs. The 1856 log cabin owned by the Thornberry family has been moved onto the railroad site and serves as a museum and store, open free every day in summer and fall and on spring weekends.

Don't worry, the engineers know just how to take turns at this pass on the Yosemite Mt. Sugar Pine Railroad.

Yosemite National Park

Enter through Fish Camp on Highway 41, El Portal on Highway 140, or Highway 120 (this road to Tioga Pass is closed during the winter, which may last until May). Visitors Center: (209) 372-0299. Daily 8–6 and 9–5 in spring and fall and on winter weekends, weather permitting. Museum open daily in summer only. Cars $5 a day.

If you and your family had only one sight to see in California, your best choice would be Yosemite National Park. Yosemite is one of the world's wonders, a world within itself. Elevations range from less than 2,000 to over 13,000 feet, and, in these 11,000 feet, five different plant belts exist. Each sustains a part of the park's wildlife population of 220 bird and 75 mammal species. In this natural splendor, you can hike, swim, camp, fish, ski, ride horseback or burro, bicycle, or simply wonder.

Your first stop should be the Visitors Center in Yosemite Valley, where you can learn about the park from the center's pamphlets, exhibits, audio-visual programs, lectures, and guided walks. The Yosemite Guide, free, at entrance stations, gives the latest schedules. There are fireside programs for youngsters.

Where you go in Yosemite will, of course, depend on your time, interests, and the time of year. You can choose from mountains, giant sequoia groves, towering waterfalls like Bridal Veil, and breathtaking vistas of Sentinal Rock and El Capitan.

There are also museums in Yosemite for rainy days or a change of pace. The **Indian Cultural Center** near the Visitors Center is of interest. Be sure to go through the self-guiding reconstruction of the **Ahwaneechee Indian village** (9–12:45 and 2–5:30 daily). The **Roundhouse** used to be the center of tribal ceremonies, and culture and crafts demonstrations are given regularly (for tours call 209-683-3631). At the **Pioneer Yosemite History Center** at Wawona, you can wander through a collection of horse-drawn vehicles, an old jail, a miner's hut, a working wagon shop, and a covered bridge. Old-time crafts demonstrations of soap making, rail splitting, and spinning are fun, and you can talk to costumed historian-interpreters, who portray the original occupants of the cabins representing the different stages in the development of Yosemite National Park.

The **Yosemite Travel Museum,** in the administration area near Arch Rock entrance, tells the story of early-day railroad and auto transportation in the region. It has a caboose, a locomotive, and a couple of cars on the grounds. The **Geology Museum** at the Visitors Center in Yosemite Valley shows how the mountains, waterfalls, and gorges were formed. The natural history of the area is also explored at the **Happy Isles Nature Center,**

The wonders of nature are an awe-
inspiring challenge to young and old,
hikers and riders, in winter and in
summer, at Yosemite National Park.

which is very youth oriented, with Junior Ranger programs, dioramas, and interactive displays.

Yosemite is overcrowded in summer, so aim to go at other times, if possible. For information about the park, write to Superintendent, Yosemite National Park, CA 95389, or telephone (209) 372-0299. Camp reservations may be made through Ticketron or 372-0307. Hotel reservations are a must. Call (209) 252-4848 or contact Yosemite Park and Curry Company, Yosemite National Park, CA 95389. For road and weather information, call (209) 372-0300. General information, recorded: 372-0265, live: 372-0265; 8–5 weekdays.

Yosemite by Air is one way to see it all. One-and-one-half-hour tours leave from Fresno Air Terminal, $69 per person, $49 for ages 5–11. One-and-a-quarter-hour tours leave from Mariposa ($59 and $45). Five-hour tours out of and back to Fresno cover everything ($99 and $75). Call (800) 622-8687 or (209) 255-8900, or write Golden Eagle Air tours, 4955 East Anderson No. 109, Fresno, CA 93727.

Bodie State Historic Park
Bodie (13 miles east of Highway 395; 7 miles south of Bridgeport). Not accessible in winter. $3 per passenger vehicle, $30 per bus. Smoking in parking lot only.

Nestled high in sagebrush country, Bodie has escaped all the commercialism often found in ghost towns. The 170 original buildings that still stand are maintained in a state of arrested disintegration: neither restored nor allowed to decay further. You walk by the 1878 Methodist church, the windowless jail, a frame schoolhouse, a small home that belonged to President Herbert Hoover's brother, the morgue with caskets still on view, and the iron vault of the bank, which was the scene of many exciting holdups. Information comes from a self-guiding tour pamphlet stowed, in summer, at the entrance station. Just wander through this quiet, ramshackle town and imagine all the high adventures that occurred here more than a century ago.

North Central California

Sutter and Colusa counties, in the north central and northeastern part of the state, comprise the most rugged, remote part of Northern California.

This area offers many unique and extraordinary sights. Lava Beds National Monument, Modoc National Forest, and Lassen Volcanic National Park are snowed-in in winter and blazingly hot in summer. Distances between towns are long, so be sure to arrange overnight camping or lodging before you set out. Nature lovers will enjoy the Whiskeytown-Lake Shasta-Trinity area and McArthur Burney Falls Memorial State park—and all the wonderful open spaces whose inaccessibility leaves them unspoiled.

Community Memorial Museum
1333 Butte House Road, Yuba City. (From Sacramento take Highway 99 north, turn left in Yuba City at the 99/20 intersection, then turn right at Civic Center Boulevard and right onto Butte House Road). (916) 674-0461. Monday–Friday 9–5 Saturday 1–4. Free.

This small community museum uses local artifacts—from baskets and grinding pots to antique pianos and dishes—to celebrate and explain the life and times of Sutter County. Experience life in Sutter County from the first Maidu Indian inhabitants and the settlement of John Sutter at Hock Farm, to the "civilization" of the county and its agricultural development. Changing exhibits reflect the diverse interests of Sutter County today.

In Marysville, Yuba's sister city, an 1857 family residence has become the **Mary Aaron Memorial Museum**, with the original furniture and clothing and an interesting display of dolls, documents, and photos. Our favorite: the 1860s wedding cake that was discovered perfectly intact and petrified in a wooden Wells Fargo storage box (704 D Street; Tuesday–Saturday 1:30–4:30, and by appointment; free; 916-743-1004).

On the levee of the river, the **Bok Kai Temple** is a 1879 Chinese temple for the river god of good fortune (D Street; 743-6501; by appointment).

Sacramento Valley Museum
1495 E. Street, Highway 20 at Interstate 5, Williams. (916) 473-2978. April–November: Wednesday–Saturday 10–4, Sunday 1–4. Winter: Friday and Saturday 10–4, Sunday 1–4, and by appointment. Adults $1; children 6–16, 25¢. Picnic area.

This 21-room museum has captured the past with a general store, a blacksmith shop and saddlery, an apothecary shop, a barber shop, and restored Early California rooms filled with memories. The double cradle from the

1700s is special. The doll collection dates from ancient Greek times, and there's an 1800 newspaper reporting George Washington's death.

Oroville Chinese Temple
1500 Broderick, Oroville. (916) 538-2496. Friday–Tuesday 11–4:30; also Wednesday and Thursday 1–4:30 in summer. Ages 12 and over, $1.50. Groups by appointment, $1.

This complex of Buddhist, Taoist, and Confucian temples houses one of the finest collections of Chinese artifacts in the United States. At the door of one building stands a two-ton cast-iron urn given to the temple by Emperor Quong She. Carved teakwood altars, old tapestries, gods and goddesses, dragons, rare lanterns, and shrines decorate the buildings. The Moon Temple, used for Buddhist worship, is entered through a circular doorway, which symbolizes the circle of life. The arts and lives of the thousands of Chinese who migrated to the goldfields are reflected in this peaceful spot.

Nearby is the **Lott House Museum.** Once the home of Judge C. F. Lott, this 19th-century house is furnished with period pieces and Early American art (1607 Montgomery Street; 916-538-2497; same hours and prices as Chinese Temple).

The Oroville Pioneer Museum, farther up Montgomery Street, is a grand collection of pioneer memorabilia, including early typewriters, an old fire engine, pictures of the Oroville floods, and a replica of a miner's cabin (916-534-0198; Sunday 1–4, and by appointment; donation).

Feather River Fish Hatchery and Oroville Dam
5 Table Mountain Boulevard, Oroville. (916) 538-2222. Hatching 8–6 daily. Dam overlook (538–2219): 8 a.m. to 9 p.m., May–September; 8–8 October and November; 8–5 December–April. Free.

A large window in the hatcher enables visitors to see the salmon climb the fish ladder to spawn (usually) in September and October. Over 10,000 salmon and steelhead live here. Ten miles up the road, you can get a good view of the 770-foot dam across the Feather River.

Bidwell Mansion

525 Esplanade, Chico. (916) 895-6144. Daily 10–4 except holidays. 45-minute tours every hour on the hour. Adults $1.

Rancho del Arroyo Chico, covering 26,000 acres, was purchased in 1849 by agriculturist and politician John Bidwell. His large Victorian home soon became the social and cultural center of the upper Sacramento Valley. Bidwell's is a California success story. He arrived in California in 1841, worked as a clerk for John Sutter, rose to the rank of general in the Mexican War, and then on July 4, 1848, struck it rich at Bidwell Bar. He set himself up in Chico and built a model farm. He raised corn, oats, barley, peaches, pears, apples, figs, quince, almonds, walnuts, wheat, olives, and cassaba melons. He was elected state senator and congressman, and even ran for President. Visitors may walk through the graciously furnished rooms. Children will like the cabinet of stuffed birds in the general's office and the intricate Victorian hair wreaths in the parlor. Bidwell Park, fourth-largest municipal park in the nation, is also part of the Bidwell estate.

The nearby **Stansbury Home**, an 1883 Italianate Victorian filled with period furnishings, is remarkable because only Stansburys have lived in it and it has never been remodeled or modernized (Fifth and Salem; 343-4401, ext. 236; weekends 1–4, and by appointment; adults 75¢, children 50¢).

South Shasta Lines

G. A. Humann Ranch, 8620 Holmes Road, Gerber. Off Highway 99. (916) 385-1389. Open even-numbered years in April and May on Sunday 12–4. Adults $3; under 12, $2.

A ¼-inch-scale model railroad based on the Southern Pacific, Gerber to Dunsmuir, under construction for 34 years by the Humann family, runs 15 steam locomotives and 100 cars on an 840-foot track. There are 1,200 miniature trees, 700 people, and 200 animals on this detailed miniature system. In addition, a real steam locomotive takes visitors for a mile-long ride.

William B. Ide Adobe State Historic Park

One mile north of Red Bluff on Adobe Road. (916) 527-5927. Park open 8–5 for picnics and fishing. Adobe open 12–4 and by appointment. Free. W.

No. 12, the famous Blue Bonnet, glides swiftly over the Cottonwood Underpass. The area is modeled exactly as the prototype before the advent of the freeway. The train is completely detailed inside and carries a load of 100 tiny passengers.

"He hereby invites all good and patriotic citizens in California to assist him—to establish and perpetuate a liberal, a just and honorable government, which shall secure to all civil, religious and personal liberty." So wrote William B. Ide to introduce the Bear Flag Republic to California. As first President of the Bear Flag Republic, he brought California into the Union. But when the Republic failed, Ide went to the goldfields and then returned home to his adobe, which also served as a ferry station between Sacramento and Shasta's northern gold mines. The house is small and unassuming, with family photos, a cradle and high chair, a furnished kitchen, and an unusual sleeping house with covered wagons, buggies, and Ide's branding equipment, are also open to the public. Two 300-year-old oaks mark the way to another small museum that includes gold-mining tools, an old button collection, and a well-used cribbage board. The Visitors Center display panels help explain the exhibits.

In Red Bluff, **The Kelly-Griggs House Museum** is open for old-house

Families get into the swing of things during a Living History Program at William B. Ide State Park.

buffs (311 Washington Street; 916-527-1129; Thursday–Sunday 2–5; donation).

Tehama-Colusa Fish Facilities
For information write P.O. Box 1050, Tyler Road, Red Bluff, CA 96080. (916) 527-7440. Spawning channels are on Tyler Road and open 8–3:30 weekdays. Camp, picnic, and boat at the Red Bluff Dam and Recreation Area, end of Sale Lane in Red Bluff; free.

The U.S. Bureau of Reclamation has created this spawning channel to aid the valley's irrigation and to encourage salmon propagation. Visitors may see king salmon on their way to upstream spawning grounds at the Salmon Viewing Plaza near the Diversion Dam in the Red Bluff Recreation Area. The best time to visit is October through December.

Carter House Natural Science Museum
Caldwell Park, 1701 Rio Drive (Highway 299 to Market Street), Redding. (916) 225-4125. Tuesday–Sunday 10–5. Free.

Did you know that tarantulas enjoy walking along your arm? In the animal discovery section of this lively science museum, you can pet a tarantula—or a possum or a ground squirrel. Native animals that are injured—sparrow hawks, screech owls, California king snakes—and domestic animals are cared for here. Bask in the sunlight of the Coggins Greenhouse/Solarium and learn about solar energy principles. Programs such as hikes and science classes keep the place busy.

Redding Museum and Art Center
1911 Rio Drive, Caldwell Park, Redding (916) 225-4155. June–August: 10–5 Tuesday–Saturday; September–May: Tuesday–Friday 12–5, Saturday 10–5. Closed holidays. Free.

Pomo Indian basketry—from cradle to pots, dresses, luggage, and houses, to gifts for the funeral pyre—is one of the excellent exhibits in this well-organized center. The permanent Indian and primitive collections include pre-Columbian pottery, canoe prows from the Trobriand Islands, and "wife beaters" from the Australian aborigines. The art galleries offer changing ex-

At Redding Museum and Art Center Children's Lawn Festival, kids learn to grind acorns, bake in a wood stove, string beads, and try a variety of other Native American, pioneer, and artistic activities.

hibits of contemporary artists, and collections of dolls, carousel animals, and quilts.

Waterworks Park
151 North Boulder Drive, Redding. (916) 246-9550. Memorial Day to Labor Day. Call for times and prices. Group rates.

Beat the heat and cure those summertime blues with the wildest, wettest time of your life. Three giant twisting, turning serpentine water slides, a 400-foot wild-whitewater inner tube river ride, a children's aquatic playground with fountains, slides and pool, water volleyball, picnic grounds, and games add up to a great vacation day.

Fort Crook Museum
Fall River Mills, 75 miles up from Redding (take Highway 299 east.) (916) 336-5710. Daily 12–4 (closed November 1–May 1).

There are six little buildings, including an 1884 one-room schoolhouse, in this historical museum, where artifacts reflect the history of the area. Old farm machinery, buggies, an old fire hose, baskets, a dugout canoe, and dolls all attract youngsters. (A reader, Elizabeth Monlux of Concord, was kind enough to tell us about this place.)

Shasta State Historic Park
Highway 299 west of Redding, Old Shasta. (916) 243-8194. Daily 10–5. Adults $1, children 50¢. Picnic areas near the stagecoach and pioneer barn.

Once the center of the rich northern gold mines, Shasta is a quiet almost-ghost town now being restored. The old county courthouse contains a remarkable collection of California art, along with displays of photographs and relics of the Indians, Chinese, gold miners, and pioneers who once lived here. Modoc handicrafts, Chinese wooden pillows and money, an 1879 *Godey's Lady's Book,* and the pistol John Brown used in his raid at Harper's Ferry are among the highlights. The courtroom is furnished as it was when in use, and the jail is still equipped with chains, leg irons, and a gallows. The Litsch General Store, open in summer, looks just as it did in the 1860s, with barrels of meat and wine, old hats, and picks and shovels for sale. Within the park are the ruins of what was once the longest row of brick buildings north of San Francisco, the town's Catholic cemetery, and other sites that are fun and safe to explore. A visitors' center complete with interpretive displays about old Shasta is in a refurbished old building across Trinity Alley from the Empire Hotel site.

J. J. (Jake) Jackson Memorial Museum and Trinity County Historical Park

508 Main Street, Highway 299 West, Weaverville. (916) 623-5211. Daily 10–5, May–October; 12–4 in April and November. Donation.

Clear displays trace Trinity County's history from the days of the Indians through the gold-mining years. Ray Jackson's collection of antique firearms, Chinese tong war weapons, a reconstructed miner's cabin, a stamp mill, and a blacksmith shop helps to recall this bygone era.

Weaverville Chinese Joss House

Main Street, 299 West, Weaverville. (916) 623-5284. Daily 10–5 except holidays. Closed Tuesday and Wednesday, November 1 to February 28. Adults $1, children 50¢.

The Temple of the Forest and the Clouds is open for worship now, as it has been since 1853, and there are tours every hour on the hour in winter, and on the half hour in summer. A small museum offers Chinese art, mining tools, weapons used in the tong wars, and photos of Chinese laborers building the railroads. A Lion Dance headdress, an abacus, opium pipes, and a huge gong are also shown. Inside the temple, you an see the paper money that is burned for the gods, and the drum and bell that wakes the gods so they'll hear your prayers. In the rear of the temple, the attendant's quarters are furnished as they were hundreds of years ago, with bunk beds and wooden pillows. Colorful altars, temple saints, celebration drums and flags, and the king's mirror-covered umbrella that guarded him against evil spirits create a vivid picture of the religion and its people.

Ironside Museum

Hawkins Bar, on Highway 299 West near Burnt Ranch. Star Route, P.O. Box 3, Hawkins Bar, CA 95525. (916) 629-2396. By chance or appointment. Donation.

Ray Nachand shares his personal collection "whenever anyone wants to see it—if we're home." Pioneer artifacts include butter churns, doctor's instruments, a collection of 200 padlocks, a glass insulator collection, Mrs. Nachand's carnival glass collection, and high-button shoes. Assaying equipment, mining equipment, machinery, and a blacksmith shop share the bill with a complete dentist's outfit. If you call before you visit, Mr. Nachand will bring out his gun and gold collections, too. Right now, he's restoring a Pelton wheel when he's not mining.

Hoopa Tribal Museum
Hoopa Valley Indian Reservation, Highway 96 (off Highway 299 West), Hoopa. (916) 625-4110. Monday–Friday 9–5. Free.

Stone implements, dishes, tools, baskets, and dance regalia of the Hoopa Indians—named by Jedediah Smith's Yurok guide as "the people who live up the river"—are shown here, along with items from other tribes, such as Kachina dolls from the Southwest, and Alaskan and Canadian baskets. Many of the Hoopa items are on loan from local residents, for this is a living museum of artifacts still used regularly in traditional tribal ceremonies. A marvelous crystal discovered in a nearby stream is now being analyzed and dated.

Shasta Dam
Highway 15 off Interstate 5. (916) 275-1587/244-1554. Daily in summer, 7:30–4. Free.

Deer come to be fed by hand when the lights shine on Shasta Dam at night. During the day, the 602-foot dam, second highest in the world, is an even more spectacular sight. Snow-capped Mount Shasta (which the athletic can climb) looms in the distance, accentuating the differences between natural and man made wonders. Jet-boat tours, camping, houseboating, and all kinds of water sports are popular in this Shasta-Whiskeytown-Trinity National Recreation Area. *Scott's Museum*, in Trinity Center, is open from 10–5 in summer, with items of local history. Children's programs and films.

A **Shasta Lake Cruise** departs from the Bay Marina north of Redding off I-5 (916-275-3021). The sternwheeler *Bridge Bay Bells* takes a two-hour cruise along Shasta's shore, past the dam and up McCloud River to Lake Shasta Caverns.

Lake Shasta Caverns
Off Lake Shasta in O'Brien. (916) 238-2341. Two-hour tours throughout the day, including a 15-minute catamaran ride across the lake; from 8 a.m. in summer, 10, 12, and 2 only in winter. Adults $9; children 4–12, $4.

Discovered in 1878 by J.A. Richardson (you can still see his inscription), the Lake Shasta Caverns are a natural wonder. Stalactite and stalagmite formations range from the eight-inch-high "ballerina" to the 60-foot "cathedral room" of stalactite draperies studded with crystals. Multicolored formations unfold before you during your tour, as you hear geological facts and Wintu Indian legends from a knowledgeable guide.

Siskiyou County Museum
910 South Main Street, Yreka. (916) 842-3836. Monday–Saturday 9–5 in summer, Tuesday–Saturday in winter. Free.

In this reproduction of the Callahan Ranch Hotel, one of the first stage stops in Siskiyou County in the 1850s, visitors learn the story of Siskiyou County from prehistoric days to the present. On the mezzanine, you'll find a parlor, bedroom, children's room, and office complete with an antique switchboard. In the basement, you'll see a country store, a milliner's shop, a music store, a blacksmith shop, a miner's cabin, and tools. A schoolhouse, a blacksmith shop, a church, an 1856 pioneer log cabin, an ore car, and a logging skid shack are on the grounds, along with many farming implements. The D.A.R. heirlooms, toys, and Mt. Shasta geodetic marker help enliven this trip to the past.

Lava Beds National Monument
Off Highway 139, near Tule Lake. (916) 667-2282. Camping $5 in summer, free in winter. Center: 8–6 in summer, 8–5 in winter. Closed Thanksgiving and Christmas.

Natural and Indian history vie for the visitors' attention in this monumental landscape of lava formations. The area abounds with natural wonders, including cinder cones that reach up to 500 feet. There are about 200 lava tube caves, which can be explored with care. Some caves hold Modoc drawings that date back centuries. Captain Jack's Stronghold, made of natural lava fortifications, is a grim reminder of later history: In 1872, Captain Jack led a band of Modoc Indians in an unsuccessful revolt against the U.S.

Cavalry, which was ending their world. This was the only major Indian war in California and is not something Americans should be proud of. A short visit to monument headquarters will help you understand the geology, natural history, and past events of the area.

Alturas Modoc County Historical Museum
600 South Main, Alturas. (916) 233-2944. Weekdays 9–4, weekends 10–4:30, May 1–November 1. Free.

To learn more about Captain Jack and see pictures of him, go to this pleasant museum in this far corner of the state. there are beads, baskets, arrowheads, and other Indian artifacts, along with pioneer memorabilia. The collections of mounted animals and birds and antique guns are popular with viewers.

Roops' Fort
75 North Weatherlow Street, Susanville. (916) 257-5721. Daily 10–4, May 15–November 15. Free.

Lassen Country memorabilia, farming and lumbering machinery, artifacts of the Native Americans, and remembrances of the first settlers, Isaac Roops and Peter Lassen, fill this interesting museum. You can peek through the fence of Roops' Fort next door, built in 1854, the first in Lassen County, to see wagonwheels from the Donner Party. Susanville is named after the daughter of Isaac Roops, governor of the provisional territory of Nevada and Nataqua.

Lassen Volcanic National Park
Highway 36, Mineral. (916) 595-4444. Information centers at Manzanita Lake and Sulphur Works open from early June to late September. Road closed in winter.

Among the attractions in this rugged area are hot springs, boiling pools, mud pots, sparkling lakes, and the cinder cone that erupted in 1851. An Indian lore program at Manzanita Lake Visitor Information Center presents the story and customs of the Native Americans who once lived here. Other programs are scheduled irregularly. *Subway Cavern,* north of Manzanita

Roop's Fort keeps its eternal, lonely vigil in the far reaches of the state.

Lake on old Highway 44 toward North Birney, just outside the park, is also worth a trip. One note of warning: The grounds and thermal areas are treacherous, so keep hold of your children at all times. Lassen Peak erupted for seven years beginning in 1914, and it's still considered active. Remember—the hydrothermal caves are named Devil's Kitchen, Sulphur Works, and Bumpass Hell for good reason.

Special Annual Events

The following annual festivals and events are listed by month and in the order they usually happen within each month. Call the local Chamber of Commerce or consult the local paper for particulars.

January

San Francisco Sports and Boat Show, Cow Palace
San Mateo Auto Show, Fairgrounds
Harlem Globe Trotters, Oakland Coliseum
Golden Gate Kennel Club All-Breed Dog Show, San Francisco
Four-Dog Sled Races, Prosser Lake and Donner Lake
Whale watching begins, Point Reyes National Seashore
Fiddlers' Contest and Crab Cioppino Feed, Cloverdale

February

Chinese New Year's Celebration, San Francisco
National Road Show, Oakland Coliseum
Crab Festival, Crescent City
Crab Feast, Bodega Bay
Redwood Region Logging Conference, Eureka
Chinese Bomb Day, Bok Kai Festival, Marysville
Cloverdale Citrus Fair
Clam Beach Run, Trinidad
Carnival and Spring Fair, Lakeport
California Special Olympics Water Games, Sonora

March

Snowfest, Lake Tahoe
Camellia Show, Santa Rosa
Crab Feed, Ukiah
Draggin' Wagons Dance Festival, Sonora
Sierra Dogsled Races, Sierra City, Truckee, and Ebbets Pass
Candlefishing at night, Klamath River
Fresno Camellia Show
Junior Grand National Livestock Expo, Cow Palace, San Francisco
Jackass Mail Run, Porterville

April

Log Race, Petaluma River
Fisherman's Festival, Bodega Bay
Baseball season opens
Annual Trinidad Crab Feed
Gem and Mineral Show, Cow Palace, San Francisco
Yacht Parade, Redwood City
Clovis Rodeo
Carmel Kite Festival
Gold Nugget Days, Paradise
Children's Lawn Festival, Redding
Red Bluff Romp and Rodeo
Coalinga Water Festival
Nikkei Matsuri Festival, San Jose
Apple Blossom Festival, Sebastopol
Fresno Folk Festival
Rhododendron Festival, Eureka
Boonville Buck-a-Roo Days
Calavaras County Jumping Frog Jubilee, Angels Camp

May

Laguna Seca Races, Monterey
Cinco de Mayo festivals in San Francisco and San Jose
Opening Day Yacht Parade, San Francisco
Ferndale Arts Festival
Avenue of the Giants Marathon, Garberville
Bay to Breakers Race, San Francisco
Luther Burbank Rose Festival, Santa Rosa
Mendocino Air Fair
Mountain Folk Festival, Potter Valley
West Coast National Antique Fly-In, Watsonville Airport
Salinas Valley Fair, King City
West Coast Relays, Fresno
Chamarita Festival and Parade, Half Moon Bay and Sausalito (Pentecost
   Sunday)
Old Settler's Day, Campbell
Fireman's Muster, Columbia
Lamb Derby Days, Willow
Russian River Wine Festival, Healdsburg
Stump Town Days and Rodeo, Guerneville
Coarsegold Rodeo, Madera County
Fiddletown Gold Country Howdown
Prospector's Daze, Willow Creek

June

Black Bart Celebration, Redwood Valley
Sonoma/Marin Fair, Petaluma Fairgrounds
Upper Grant Avenue Street Fair, San Francisco
Dipsea Race, Mill Valley
Midsummer Music Festival, Stern Grove, San Francisco
Highway 50 Wagon Train, Placerville
Secession Day, Rough and Ready (June 27)
San Francisco's Birthday Celebration

At the Annual Spring Faire in Healdsburg,
a puppet show entertains children of all
ages.

July

Old Time Fourth of July Celebration, Columbia
Salmon B-B-Q, Noyo
Sonoma County Fair, Santa Rosa
C.B. Radio Convention, Eureka
Bach Festival, Carmel
California Rodeo, Salinas
Nihon Machi Street Fair, Japantown, San Francisco
Asian Festival, Oakland Museum
Hoopa Fourth of July Celebration, Hoopa
Pony Express Celebration, Pollack Pines
Napa County Fair, Calistoga (July 4)
Willits Frontier Days (July 4)
Arcata Salmon Festival
Mendota Sugar Festival
Garberville Rodeo
Folsom Rodeo

San Mateo County Fair
Woodminster Music Series, Oakland (through September)
San Francisco Fair and Exposition
Hangtown Festival, Placerville
Sacramento Water Festival
Carnival, San Francisco
Fly-In and Moonlight Flight, Placerville
Alameda County Fair, Pleasanton
Merienda, Monterey's birthday party
San Antonio Mission Fiesta, Jolon
Springfest, San Mateo Fairgrounds
Old Auburn Flea Market
Italian Picnic and Parade, Sutter Creek
Klamath Salmon Barbecue
Shasta Bridge Jamboree, Redding
Malakoff Homecoming, Nevada City
Solano County Fair, Vallejo
Novato County Fair
Pony Express Days, McKinleyville
Garberville Rodeo and Western Celebration
Father's Day Kite Festival, San Francisco
Bear Flag Day, Sonoma
Tuolumne Jubilee, Tuolumne City
Kit Carson Days, Jackson
Butterfly Days, Mariposa
Cornish Miner's Picnic, Grass Valley
Fiddler's Jamboree, Railroad Flat
Bonanza Days, Gilroy
Redwood Acres Fair, Eureka
Western Daze, Fairfield Western Weekend, Novato
Vaquero Days, Hollister
Horse Show and Rodeo, San Benito
Old-Fashioned Fourth, Mount Shasta
Old-Fashioned Fourth, Crescent City
Dune Daze, Samoa
Grand Comedy Festival, Eureka
Fortuna Rodeo
Water Carnival, Monte Rio
Jeepers Jamboree, Georgetown to Lake Tahoe
Fiesta Rodeo de San Juan Bautista
Captain Weber Days, Stockton

Obon Festival, Monterey
Obon Festival, Fresno
Scotts Valley Days
Gold Rush Jubilee, Callahan, Siskiyou County
Feast of Lanterns, Pacific Grove
Orick Rodeo
Easter Lily Festival, Smith River
Gasket Raft Races
Turtle Races, Cloverdale
Nightboat Parade, Lakeport and Clearlake Highlands
Marin County Fair, San Rafael

August

Old Adobe Days, Petaluma
Monterey County Fair
Humboldt County Fair, Ferndale
California State Horseman's American Horse Show, Sonoma
Annie and Mary Day, Blue Lake
Santa Clara County Fair, San Jose
Indian Fair Days, Sierra Mono Museum, North Fork
Gilroy Garlic Festival
Wildwood Days and Peddlers' Fair, Rio Dell
Siskiyou County Fair and Paul Bunyan Jubilee, Yreka
Ringling Brothers Circus, Oakland
Calamari Festival, Santa Cruz
Jamestown Pioneer Days
El Dorado Days at Mt. Ranch, San Andreas
Mother Lode Fair and Loggers' Contest, Sonora
Plumas County Fair, Quincy
Pony Express Day, McKinleyville (August 22)
Children's Fairytale Birthday Week, Oakland
Air Round-Up, Red Bluff
Del Norte County Fair, Crescent City
Gravenstein Apple Fair, Sebastopol
Lake County Fair, Lakeport
Renaissance Pleasure Faire, Novato (to September)

September

Sausalito Art Festival
Begonia Festival, Capitola
Monterey Jazz Festival
Mendocino County Fair and Apple Show, Boonville
Ringling Brothers Circus, San Francisco
San Francisco Art Festival
Fall Festival, Japantown, San Francisco
Redwood Empire Logging Festival, McKinleyville
Constitution Days, Nevada City
Vintage Festival, Hall of Flowers, Golden Gate Park, San Francisco
California State Fair, Sacramento
Scottish Games, Santa Rosa Fairgrounds
Columbia Admission Day
Pageant of Fire Mountain, Guerneville
Vintage Car Fair, Fremont
National Indian Observance Day, Crescent City
American Indian Pow Wow, Volcano
Paul Bunyan Days, Fort Bragg
Concord Jazz Festival
Indian "Big Time" Days, Amador County
Santa Cruz County Fair, Watsonville
Vintage Festival, Sonoma
North Country Fair, Arcata
Carmel Mission Fiesta
Fiesta del Pueblo, San Jose
Redwood Invitational Regatta, Big Lagoon, Humboldt County
Oktoberfest, San Mateo Fairgrounds
Oktoberfest, San Jose
Lodi Grape Festival
Fiesta Patrias, Woodland
Castroville Artichoke Festival
Walnut Festival, Walnut Creek
Sonoma Valley of the Moon Festival
Sourdough Days, Sutter Hill
Weaverville Bigfoot Daze

October

Laguna Seca Grand Prix, Monterey
Fortuna Arts Festival
Sonoma County Harvest Festival, Santa Rosa
Fresno Fair
National Livestock Expo, Cow Palace, San Francisco
Marin Grape Festival, San Rafael
Pumpkin Festival, Half Moon Bay
Football season starts
Spanishtown Art and Pumpkin Festival
Columbia Fiddle and Banjo Contest
Candle Lighter Ghost House, Fremont
Pro-Am Surfing International, Santa Cruz
Redding Children's Art Festival
Fall Festival, Clearlake Oaks
Selma Parade and Band Festival
Blessing of the Fleet, San Francisco
Johnny Appleseed Day, Paradise
Lumberjack Day, West Point
Harbor Festival, Morro Day
Great Sand Castle Building Contest, Carmel
Great Snail Race, Folsom
Oktoberfest, Tahoe City
Old Timers' Day, King City
Columbus Day Festival, San Francisco
Reedley Festival
Chinese Double Ten Celebration, San Francisco
San Francisco International Film Festival
Discovery Day, Bodega Bay
Harvest Hoedown, Healdsburg

November

North California Boat and Sports Show, Oakland
Christmas Balloon Parade, San Jose (day after Thanksgiving)
Thanksgiving Art Fair, Mendocino

December

Christmas Art and Music Festival, Eureka
Great Dickens Faire, San Francisco
Nutcracker Suite, San Francisco Ballet
Nutcracker Suite, Oakland Ballet
Festival of the Trees, Monterey
Festival of the Trees, San Rafael
Shriners East-West Football Game, Candlestick Park, San Francisco
    (December 31)
Lighting of the Tree of Lebanon, Santa Rosa
New Year's Eve Fireman's Ball, Cloverdale
Natives' Christmas Tree Ceremony, Sequoia National Park
Christmas Tree Lane, Fresno
Pioneer Christmas Party, Ide Adobe, Red Bluff
Rice-Pounding Ceremony, Japantown, San Francisco
Miner's Christmas Columbia
Amador Calico Christmas
San Juan Bautista de Posada Fiesta
Victorian Christmas, Nevada City
St. Nicholas in the Barnyard, Carmel Valley

Index

After living in New York City for thirty years, **Elizabeth Pomada** moved to San Francisco. She learned about Northern California by traveling over four thousand miles of it to write *Places to Go with Children in Northern California.* Her other books include *California Publicity Outlets,* now published as *Metro California Media; Painted Ladies: San Francisco's Resplendent Victorians; Daughters of Painted Ladies: America's Resplendent Victorians;* the new *How to Create Your Own Painted Lady;* and, soon, *Painted Ladies Revisited: San Francisco Inside and Out.* With her partner, Michael Larsen, she runs a literary agency in San Francisco.

Photo Credits:

Thanks to the following people and organizations for providing the photographs used in this book:

Mark E. Gibson, cover; Redwood Empire Association, x, 4, 6, 8, 16, 30, 32, 33, 37, 98, 114, 115, 116, 117, 122, 125, 128, 129, 131, 132; Michael F. Larsen, 40, 42, 83, 132, 135, 142, 147, 152, 154, 160, 161, 164, 175, 176; Court Mast, 12, 13; Edward R. Susse, 23, 34; San Francisco Exploratorium, 24, 25; San Francisco Zoo, 27, 28; Oakland Zoo, 45, 46; Lynne Calonico, Lawrence Hall of Science, 47; Jeff Weissman, Alta Bates Hospital, 49; Angela Pancrazio, Hayward Area Historical Society, 50; San Mateo County Historical Association, 59; Ernest Braun, Coyote Point Museum, 60, 61; California History Center, 65; Rosicrucian Order, 69, 70; Happy Hollow Park, 72, Monterey Bay Aquarium, 76, 86, 87. Santa Cruz Beach Boardwalk, 79; Santa Cruz City Museum, 80; Roaring Camp, 82; Fred Capen, Pacific Grove Museum of Natural History, 92; Charles M. Bancroft, State Park Ranger, Point Lobos, 95; Old Faithful Geyser, 103; Petaluma Chamber of Commerce, 105; The Creamery, 106; Winner's Circle, 107; State of California Department of Parks & Recreation, 108; California Western Railroad, 120. Marine World/Africa USA, 134; Crocker Art Museum, 140; Harre W. Demoro, Western Railway Museum, 146; Mercer Caverns, 156; Edwards Studio, Zalud House, 171; Joseph T. Bispo, Yosemite Mt. Sugar Pine Railroad, 180; John Poimiroo, Yosemite Park & Curry Co., 176; South Shasta Photo, 187; William B. Ide Adobe State Park, 188; Richard Ray, Redding Museum & Art Center, 190; Eastman's Studio, Roop's Fort, 196; Healdsburg Chamber of Commerce, 200.